MW00824486

Mountain Dew Cookbook:

150+ Dang Good MNT DEW Recipes that Use the Lemon-Lime Drink in Ways You've Never Seen Before

TABLE OF CONTENTS

INTRODUCTION **6**

DANG GOOD BREAKFAST RECIPES **7**

1. Breakfast Pudding Filled With Chia 7
2. Bowls Of Mexican Taste 8
3. Almond & Squash Snack 8
4. Cauliflower Mix Quick Meal 9
5. Cup In Taco 9
6. Faro Salad With Arugula 10
7. Feta Cheese Salad 11
8. Fresh Strawberry Salsa 11
9. Goat Cheese Salad 12
10. Panera Mediterranean Breakfast Sandwich 12
11. Mediterranean Breakfast Wraps 13
12. Breakfast Enchiladas 14
13. Mediterranean Breakfast Quinoa 15
14. Chickpea & Potato Hash 16
15. Spaghetti Frittata 17
16. Hearty Breakfast Frittata With Tomato Salad 17
17. Breakfast Quesadilla 18
18. Roquefort Pear Toast 19
19. Chickpea Salad 20
20. Hot Shrimp Avocado Salad 20
21. Middle East Rice Salad 21
22. Sardou Eggs 22

DANG GOOD SNACK RECIPES **24**

23. Tomato Zoodle Salad 24
24. Dill Topped Squash And Cucumber Mix 25
25. Seasoned Okra With Tomatoes 25
26. Savory Celery Stir-Fry 26
27. Easy Celery And Squash Jumble 26
28. Creamy Polenta 27
29. Crispy Corn 27

30. Cucumber Yogurt Salad With Mint 28

31. Curry Wheatberry Rice 28

32. Couscous Salad 29

33. Cool Garbanzo And Spinach Beans 30

34. Citrus Couscous With Herb 30

35. Cilantro And Avocado Platter 31

36. Cauliflower Broccoli Mash 31

37. Caramelized Pears And Onions 32

38. Parsnips With Tahini Dressing 32

39. Seasoned Green Beans 33

40. Baked Garlic Ricotta 33

41. Whiting Bread With Sesame 34

42. Crab Montage With Mushroom Soup 35

43. Number 0Baked Sole With Cauliflower Salad 36

DANG GOOD SEA FOOD RECIPES **37**

44. Tasty Fish Curry 37

45. Easy Cod 38

46. Pan-Fried Cod With Saffron 38

47. Rosemary Flounder 39

48. Stuffed Oysters 39

49. Seared Sea Scallops 40

50. Salmon Cakes With Lemon Caper Sauce 40

51. Classic Lobster Salad 41

52. Buttery Lobster Tails 42

53. Simply Shrimp 43

54. Crab Cakes With Arugula And Blackberry Salad 43

55. Steamer Clams 44

56. Oysters Rockefeller 45

57. Crab-Stuffed Mushrooms 45

58. Salmon and Chive Pate 46

59. Creole Red Fish Bites 47

60. Blackened Potato Crusted Shrimp 48

61. Crispy Oysters 48

62. Cajun Bbq Shrimps 49

63.	Southern Stuffed Artichokes	49
64.	Number 0louisiana Shrimp Boil	50
65.	Number 0 Cornmeal Crusted Catfish With Lemon-Thyme Mayo	51
66.	Crawfish Etouffee	52

DANG GOOD MEAT AND POULTRY RECIPES 54

67.	Greek Penne And Chicken	54
68.	Yogurt-Marinated Chicken Kebabs	55
69.	Crispy Mediterranean Chicken Thighs	55
70.	High-Quality Belizean Chicken Stew	56
71.	Garlic And Lemon Chicken Dish	57
72.	Honey Balsamic Chicken	57
73.	Chicken Shawarma	58
74.	Buffalo-Style Pork Meatballs	59
75.	Peach Barbecue Pork Chops	60
76.	Flank Steak With Creamy Horseradish Sauce	60
77.	T-Bone With Garlic Rosemary Compound Butter	61
78.	Grilled Chicken Cobb Salad	62
79.	Fried Artichoke Hearts	63
80.	Kedgeree	63
81.	Chicken And Lemon Casserole	64
82.	Skewers Of Seitan	65
83.	Chicken Soup	65

DANG GOOD SAUCES 67

84.	Sautéed Shrimp	67
85.	Chunky Avocado Sauce	68
86.	Green Salsa	68
87.	Smoky Hot Bbq Sauce	69
88.	Mojo Sauce	70
89.	Southwestern Squash Sauce	71
90.	New Mexican Chili Sauce	72
91.	Everyday Barbecue Sauce	73
92.	Forest Berry Sauce	73
93.	Silky White Wine Sauce	74
94.	Coconut Milk Sauce	75

95. Peanut Sauce 76

96. Carbohydrates 11 77

97. Lemongrass Curry 78

98. Dipping Fish Sauce 79

99. Apple Sauce Treat 80

100. Avocado And Egg Sandwich 80

101. Tahini Dip 81

102. Homemade Ginger Dressing 81

103. Homemade Lemon Vinaigrette 82

104. Homemade Ranch 82

105. Honey Bean Dip 83

106. Soy With Honey And Ginger Glaze 84

107. Cucumber And Dill Sauce 84

108. Dairy-Free Creamy Turmeric Dressing 85

109. Herby Raita 85

110. Creamy Avocado Dressing 86

111. Creamy Homemade Greek Dressing 87

112. Bean Potato Spread 87

113. Cashew Ginger Dip 88

114. Almond Pear Express Cream 88

115. Red Pepper Chickpea Dip 89

DANG GOOD DESSERTS **90**

116. Baked Fennel 90

117. Madeira Cake 91

118. Lemon Cheesecake 91

119. Easy Fish Cakes 92

120. Chocolate Pear Charlotte 93

121. Peach Fondant 94

122. Lemon Tassies 94

123. Number 0 Crab Cakes 95

DANG GOOD DRINKS AND COCKTAILS **97**

124. Raspberries For Recovery 97

125. Tomato Fresca Cooler 98

126. Holiday Punch 98

127. Southern Almond Tea 99

128. Southern Lemon Iced Tea 100

129. FIVE BONUS Mnt Dew Drink Recipes! 101

130. Arctic Mouthwash Ice 101

131. Ass-Smacker 101

132. Captain Dew 102

133. Dew Driver 102

DANG GOOD ICE CREAM **103**

134. Ginger Pear Sorbet 103

135. Lemonade Sorbet 104

136. Lemon Lime Soda Sorbet 104

137. Lemon Cream Ice Cream 104

138. Mascarpone Ice Cream 105

139. Red Velvet Cake Ice Cream 106

140. Raspberry Dark Chocolate Swirl Ice Cream 107

141. Banana Frozen Yogurt 107

142. Zesty Lemon Frozen Yogurt 108

143. Blueberry Frozen Yogurt 108

144. Strawberry Frozen Yogurt 109

145. Limoncello Gelato (Gelato Di Limoncello) 109

146. Fresh Fig Gelato (Gelato Di Fiche) 110

147. Black Cherry Ice Cream 110

148. Lemon Ice Cream 111

149. Italian Espresso Ice Cream 112

150. Sangria Slushies 112

151. Lemon Custard Sorbet 113

152. Plum Sorbet 114

153. Mascarpone Sorbet 115

154. Sweet Cherry Sorbet 116

155. All-Natural Pink Lemonade Sorbet 117

156. Fresh Strawberry Ice Cream 118

157. Tarragon Sorbet 119

158. Cool And Classic Lemon Sorbet 120

CONCLUSION **121**

INTRODUCTION

Have you tried cooking vegetables with the touch of lemon-lime drink in a way that you've never seen before?

Have you ever thought that there is way more to your favorite veggies besides beets?

About healthy food and nutritional recipes taken from natural sources?

It's time to find out!

After all, you've only got your mind and healthy food recipes, oh, and maybe some cool superpowers!

This story is an introduction to healthy food that will awaken the superpowers of creativity. And taste!

And most importantly, this story intends to train you to create your recipes today, believe in yourself, and don't be afraid to get creative!

The newest story for adults that promises to inspire a new level of motivation and commitment. The story features an individual who wants to restore confidence in his relationship after leaving an abusive relationship. As an avid cyclist, he loved to ride his bike but cannot go very far. He goes to a local farmer's market. There he meets some new friends that will be his motivation not to give up. They share their healthy food restaurant stories. He then begins to share his story with some of them. These individuals help him learn how to overcome the agoraphobia that left him with after the abusive relationship. This story shows how his new friends are very supportive in reaching his goal. You will find this story to be very entertaining, touching, and encouraging, and a great ending story to inspire the reader to keep moving toward his goals and values, whether they be business, career, relationship, or anything. With this fantastic book, you will be reading all about the most recent crazy and absurd ingredients in healthy food recipes, including not only vegetables but also superpowers and local background.

The daily meal we eat affects our health and welfare, and our funds play a key role in the foods we buy and prepare. This book is not only for people who wish to save money but also for anyone looking for healthy food options that are well-priced and delicious!

A few important details! The story is divided into chapters, many of them in recipes for healthy food, superhero experience, natural ideas, and real-life and relationship problems and their solutions. The author's goal was to use a style that was both consistent and clear. This story illustrates the various methods psychologists cite to resolve problem situations in relationships, be it verbal, physical, or emotional. The author used these to bring about his story. This story is an exciting, creative, believable story that Servings: to motivate the reader to be creative and healthy and motivate him to believe in himself and not give up.

What you're waiting to take your notebook and pen and start taking notes from this awesome cookbook. The recipes in this book are organic, as well as gluten-free and soy-free. It would help if you adapted this book to fit your nutrition needs for any specials that you may have to your diet. Don't wait for any further, don't let yourself down; start reading today!

DANG GOOD BREAKFAST RECIPES

1. Breakfast Pudding Filled With Chia

Preparation time: 14 minutes

Cooking time: 14 minutes

Servings: 4

INGREDIENTS:

- Coffee-2 tablespoons
- Water-2 cups
- Chia seeds-1 3 cup
- Coconut cream-1 4 cup
- Stevia-1 tablespoon
- Vanilla extract-1 tablespoon
- Sugar-free chocolate chips-2 tablespoons
- Coconut cream-1 4 cup

DIRECTIONS:

1. Take a small pot.
2. Warm it up with the water over medium heat.
3. Bring the water to a boil.
4. Mix in the coffee and simmer for 15 minutes.
5. Put that off the heat.

6. Then strain into a bowl.
7. Toss in the vanilla extract, coconut cream, stevia, chocolate chips and chia seeds.
8. Whisk in well then cover.
9. Leave it aside for 10 minutes.
10. Divide into bowls.
11. Serve cold for breakfast.
12. Enjoy!

NUTRITION: Calories 21 Fats 12g Fiber 1g Carbohydrate 5g Protein 1g

2. Bowls Of Mexican Taste

Preparation time: 13 minutes

Cooking time: 23 minutes

Servings: 7

INGREDIENTS:

- Canned green chilies-4 ounces (chopped)
- Tomatoes-3 (chopped)
- Green bell pepper-1 (chopped)
- Yellow onion-1 (chopped)
- Red bell pepper-1 (chopped)
- Oregano-1 2 teaspoon (dried)
- Chili powder-2 teaspoons
- Salt and black pepper-A pinch
- Olive oil-1 tablespoon

DIRECTIONS:

1. Take a pan and bring the oil to heat over medium heat.
2. Mix the onion, bell peppers, tomatoes, oregano, salt, pepper and chili powder.
3. Toss well and cook for 10 minutes.
4. Add the chilies.
5. Again, stir and cook for 10 minutes.
6. Divide into bowls and serve.
7. Enjoy!

NUTRITION: Calories 55 Fats 6g Fiber 4g Carbohydrate 2g Protein 3g

3. Almond & Squash Snack

Preparation time: 11 minutes

Cooking time: 12 minutes

Servings: 3

INGREDIENTS:

- Walnuts-1 4 cup (soaked for 12 hours and drained)

- Almonds-1 4 cup
- Butternut squash-1 (peeled and cubed)
- Cinnamon powder-1 teaspoon
- Stevia-1 tablespoon
- Almond milk-1 cup

DIRECTIONS:

1. Pick up a pot.
2. Put and combine the walnuts with almonds, squash, cinnamon, stevia and milk.
3. Mix well and bring it to a simmer.
4. Cook for 15 minutes then divide into bowls and serve.
5. Enjoy!

NUTRITION: Calories 153 Fats 7g Fiber 3g Carbohydrate 2g Protein 5g

4. Cauliflower Mix Quick Meal

Preparation time: 11 minutes

Cooking time: 17 minutes

Servings: 3

INGREDIENTS:

- Egg-1 (whisked)
- Salt and black pepper-A pinch
- Cauliflower florets-2 cups
- Red bell pepper-1 (chopped)
- Onion-1 tablespoon (chopped)
- Olive oil-1 2 tablespoon
- Goat cheese-1 tablespoon (crumbled)

DIRECTIONS:

1. Bring the oil to heat in a pan.
2. Put it to the oil over medium heat.
3. Combine the onion, stir and cook for 1-2 minutes.
4. Mix in the cauliflower, bell pepper, salt and pepper.
5. Stir and cook for 7 minutes.
6. Whisk the egg and the cheese.
7. Mix and cook for 2 minutes more.
8. Divide between plates and serve for breakfast.

NUTRITION: Calories 12 Fats 5g Fiber 3g Carbohydrate 2g Protein 7g

5. Cup In Taco

Preparation time: 13 minutes

Cooking time: 23 minutes

Servings: 5

INGREDIENTS:

- Celery-1 cup (peeled and cubed)
- Eggs-4
- Yellow onion-1 4 cup (chopped)
- Jalapeno-1 (chopped)
- Salt and black pepper-A pinch
- Chili powder-1 4 teaspoon
- Taco seasoning-3 4 teaspoon

DIRECTIONS:

1. Take a mixing bowl.
2. Combine the eggs with onion, jalapeno, celery, salt, pepper, chili powder and taco seasoning.
3. Mix and slide that into a casserole.
4. Then shift in the oven.
5. Bake at 380 degrees F for 20 minutes.
6. Slice the baked dish meal.
7. Divide between plates and serve for breakfast.

NUTRITION: Calories 119 Fats 8g Fiber 1g Carbohydrate 3g Protein 7g

6. Faro Salad With Arugula

Preparation Time: ten minutes

Cooking Time: thirty-five minutes

Servings: 2

INGREDIENTS:

- ½ cup faro
- ½ teaspoon ground black pepper
- ½ teaspoon Italian seasoning
- ½ teaspoon olive oil
- 1 ½ cup chicken stock
- 1 cucumber, chopped
- 1 tablespoon lemon juice
- 1 teaspoon salt
- 2 cups arugula, chopped

DIRECTIONS:

1. Mix up together faro, salt, and chicken stock and move mixture in the pan.
2. Close the lid and boil it for a little more than half an hour.
3. In the meantime, place all rest of the ingredients in the salad container.
4. Chill the faro to the room temperature and put in it in the salad container too.
5. Mix up the salad well.

NUTRITION: Calories 92 Fats 3g Fiber 2g Carbohydrate 16g Protein 4g

7. Feta Cheese Salad

Preparation Time: ten minutes

Cooking Time: 0 minutes

Servings: 2

INGREDIENTS:

- 1 tbsp. olive oil (extra virgin)
- 1 tsp balsamic vinegar
- 2 cucumbers
- 30 g feta cheese
- 4 spring onions
- 4 tomatoes
- Salt

DIRECTIONS:

1. Cube the tomatoes and cucumbers.
2. Thinly slice the onions.
3. Crush the feta cheese.
4. Mix tomatoes, onions, and cucumbers.
5. Put olive oil, vinegar, and a small amount of salt.
6. Put in feta cheese.
7. Enjoy your meal!

NUTRITION: Calories 221 Fats 14g Fiber 3g Carbohydrate 18g Protein 11g

8. Fresh Strawberry Salsa

Preparation Time: ten minutes

Cooking Time: 0 minutes

Servings: 6-8

INGREDIENTS:

- 1 4 cup fresh lime juice
- ½ cup fresh cilantro
- ½ cup red onion, finely chopped
- ½ teaspoon lime zest, grated
- 1-2 jalapeños, deseeded, finely chopped
- 2 kiwi fruit, peeled, chopped
- 2 pounds fresh ripe strawberries, hulled, chopped
- 2 teaspoons pure raw honey

DIRECTIONS:

1. Put in lime juice, lime zest and honey into a big container and whisk well.
2. Put in remaining ingredients then mix thoroughly.
3. Cover and set aside for a while for the flavors to set in and serve.

NUTRITION: Calories 119 Fats 5g Fiber 2g Carbohydrate 12 g Protein 10g

9. Goat Cheese Salad

Preparation Time: fifteen minutes

Cooking Time: thirty minutes

Servings: 4

INGREDIENTS:

- ½ cup of walnuts
- ½ head of escarole (medium), torn
- 1 bunch of trimmed and torn arugula
- 1 3 cup extra virgin olive oil
- 2 bunches of medium beets (~1 ½ lbs.) with trimmed tops
- 2 tbsp. of red wine vinegar
- 4 oz. crumbled of goat cheese (aged cheese is preferred)
- Kosher salt + freshly ground black pepper

DIRECTIONS:
1. Place the beets in water in a deep cooking pan and apply salt as seasoning. Now, boil them using high heat for approximately twenty minutes or until they're soft. Peel them off when they're cool using your fingers or use a knife.
2. To taste, whisk the vinegar with salt and pepper in a big container. Then mix in the olive oil for the dressing. Toss the beets with the dressing, so they're uniformly coated and marinate them for approximately fifteen minutes – 2 hours.
3. Set the oven to 350F. Bring the nuts on a baking sheet and toast them for approximately 8 minutes (stirring them once) until they turn golden brown. Let them cool.
4. Mix and toss the escarole and arugula with the beets and put them in four plates. Put in the walnuts and goat cheese as toppings before you serve.
5. Enjoy!

NUTRITION: Calories 285 Fats 26g Fiber 5g Carbohydrate 2g Protein 12g

10. Panera Mediterranean Breakfast Sandwich

Preparation Time: 15 minutes

Cooking Time: 5 minutes

Servings: 1

INGREDIENTS:

- 2 Egg Whites
- 1 Ciabatta Roll

- 1 slice of Tomato
- 1 slice of White Cheddar Cheese
- 1 tablespoon of Pesto
- 1 handful of Baby Spinach
- Cracked Black Pepper

DIRECTIONS:

1. Split your roll and place the cheese on bottom half.
2. Lightly broil the half of roll with cheese on it in your toaster oven.
3. Spray a ramekin or mug with cooking spray. Pour eggs whites into it and cover. Microwave for approximately 45 to 60 seconds. Place tomato slice on top of your cooked egg and microwave it for about 10 more seconds.
4. Place your cooked egg and tomato on top of your cheese covered half of roll. Sprinkle the top with cracked pepper. Spread pesto on the top half of your roll. Add spinach on top of the tomato and put your sandwich together.
5. Serve and Enjoy!

NUTRITION: Calories 45 Fats 13g Fiber 2g Carbohydrate 12g Protein 11g

11. Mediterranean Breakfast Wraps

Preparation Time: 15 minutes

Cooking Time: 5 minutes

Servings: 4

INGREDIENTS:

- 4 Eggs
- 4 Tortillas
- 1 tablespoon of Water

- 1 2 teaspoons of Garlic Chipotle Seasoning
- 4 tablespoons of Crumbled Feta Cheese
- 4 tablespoons of Tomato Chutney
- 1 cup of Chopped Fresh Spinach Leaves
- Dried Tomatoes
- Bacon
- Prosciutto
- Salt
- Pepper

DIRECTIONS:

1. Mix your eggs, seasoning, and water.
2. Heat a skillet. Add some butter or bacon grease. Add in your egg mixture and scramble for 3 to 4 minutes until cooked.
3. Lay your tortillas out and divide your eggs among them evenly. Leave the edges free so you can fold them.
4. Top each layer of your eggs with an even amount of cheese. Approximately 1 tablespoon for each wrap.
5. Add tomato chutney. Approximately 1 tablespoon for each wrap.
6. Add spinach. Approximately 1/4 cup for each wrap.
7. Add bacon and prosciutto. I use a couple of slices on each wrap but feel free to add the amount you prefer.
8. Roll up the tortilla's burrito style. Be sure to fold in both of your ends.
9. Cook approximately 1 minute on a skillet or panini maker.
10. Serve and Enjoy!

NUTRITION: Calories 35 Fats 11g Fiber 2g Carbohydrate 20g Protein 12g

12. Breakfast Enchiladas

Preparation Time: 20 minutes

Cooking Time: 5 minutes

Servings: 4

INGREDIENTS:

- 14 Large Eggs
- 8 ounces of Spicy Vegetarian Breakfast Sausages
- 2 tablespoons of Butter
- 4 Sliced Green Onions
- 2 tablespoons of Chopped Fresh Cilantro
- 1 half teaspoon of Pepper
- 3 fourth teaspoon of Salt
- 8 Whole Wheat Tortillas
- 1 cup of Shredded Pepper Jack Cheese

- 1 third cup of Flour
- 3 cups of Milk
- 1 third cup of Butter
- 2 cups of Shredded Cheddar Cheese
- 4 and half ounces of Chopped Green Chile
- 1 half cup of Grape Tomatoes
- 1 eight cups of Sliced Black Olives

DIRECTIONS:

1. Melt your butter in a saucepan over a medium heat. Whisk in the flour until it is smooth. Cook, constantly whisking for approximately 1 minute. Gradually, whisk in your milk and continue to cook over a medium heat. Whisk constantly until mixture has thickened. Should take approximately 5 minutes. Remove from heat. Whisk in your chile, cheddar cheese, and salt.
2. Cook your sausage. Remove from pan when finished. Drain if necessary.
3. Melt butter in a large skillet over a medium heat. Add in your cilantro and green onions. Sauté them. Add your salt, eggs, and pepper. Cook without any stirring until your eggs have begun to set. Bring your spatula across the bottom of your pan to help distribute uncooked eggs. Keep cooking until the eggs have gotten thick but are still moist. Remove from the heat and fold in your sausage and 1 1 2 cups of cheese sauce from the first step.
4. Spoon 1 3 of a cup of your egg mixture down the center of each of your tortillas and roll up. Place the seam side down in a greased 13 x 9 baking dish. Repeat for all your tortillas. Pour your remaining cheese mixture over the tortillas evenly and sprinkle with pepper jack cheese. Refrigerate approximately 45 minutes.
5. Bake at 350 degrees for approximately 30 minutes or until your cheese is bubbling. Sprinkle with the toppings of your choice.

NUTRITION: Calories 55 Fats 21g Fiber 4g Carbohydrate 7g Protein 32g

13. Mediterranean Breakfast Quinoa

Preparation Time: 15 minutes

Cooking Time: 10 minutes

Servings: 4

INGREDIENTS:

- 1 teaspoon of Ground Cinnamon
- 1 fourth cup of Chopped Raw Almonds
- 2 cups of Milk
- 1 cup of Quinoa
- 1 teaspoon of Vanilla Extract
- 1 teaspoon of Sea Salt
- 2 Chopped Dried Pitted Dates
- 2 tablespoons of Honey
- 5 Chopped Dried Apricots

DIRECTIONS:

1. Toast your almonds in your skillet over a medium heat. Should take approximately 3 to 5 minutes until golden. Set them aside.
2. Heat your quinoa and cinnamon together in your saucepan over a medium heat.
3. Add the sea salt and milk to your saucepan. Stir in well.
4. Bring your mixture to a boil, reduce the heat to low. Cover your saucepan and allow to simmer for approximately 15 minutes.
5. Stir in your honey, dates, vanilla, apricots, and 1 2 of your toasted almonds.
6. Pour rest of almonds on top when ready to serve.

NUTRITION: Calories 55 Fats 21g Fiber 4g Carbohydrate 7g Protein 32g

14. Chickpea & Potato Hash

Preparation Time: 20 minutes

Cooking Time: 10 minutes

Servings: 4

INGREDIENTS:

- 4 cups of Frozen Shredded Hash Brown Potatoes
- 1 half cup of Finely Chopped Onion
- 2 cups of Finely Chopped Baby Spinach
- 1 tablespoon of Minced Fresh Ginger
- 1 half teaspoon of Salt
- 1 tablespoon of Curry Powder
- 1 fourth cup of Extra-Virgin Olive Oil
- 4 Large Eggs
- 1 (15-ounce) can of Chickpeas
- 1 cup of Chopped Zucchini

DIRECTIONS:

1. Combine your spinach, potatoes, ginger, onion, salt, and curry powder in a big bowl. Heat your oil in a large sized skillet over a medium-high heat. Add in your potato mixture and press down into a layer. Cook mixture without stirring. Cook until golden brown on bottom and crispy. Should take approximately 3 to 5 minutes.
2. Reduce the heat to a medium-low. Fold in your zucchini and chickpeas. Once folded in, press your mixture back into an even layer. Carve 4 wells out in your mixture. Break your eggs, one at a time and slip into each of your wells. Cover and continue to cook until your eggs are set. Should take approximately 4 to 5 minutes.

NUTRITION: Calories 55 Fats 21g Fiber 4g Carbohydrate 7g Protein 32g

15. Spaghetti Frittata

Preparation Time: 30 minutes

Cooking Time: 30 minutes

Servings: 6

INGREDIENTS:

- 6 Large Eggs
- 2 cups of Cooked Spaghetti
- 4 slices of Bacon
- 2 cloves of Minced Garlic
- 1 Diced Purple Onion
- 1 cup of Grated Mozzarella Cheese
- 1 fourth cup of Grated Parmesan Cheese
- 3 ounces of Chopped Spinach
- 2 cloves of Minced Garlic
- 1 fourth cup of Sliced Black Olives
- 6 Grape Tomatoes
- 1 tablespoon of Fresh Basil Leaves
- Ground Black Pepper
- Salt

DIRECTIONS:

1. In a big bowl, whisk your parmesan cheese and eggs until well blended. Season with pepper and salt. Add your spaghetti and toss it so everything gets combined. Set aside.
2. Preheat your oven to 375 degrees. In a large cast iron skillet over a medium heat, cook your bacon until it is crisp and set on paper towels to drain. Add onion to your skillet and sauté over a medium heat approximately 5 minutes. Stir it often until softened. Add your spinach and cook it until it has wilted. Should take 2 minutes. Add your garlic and sauté until it becomes fragrant. Should take about 1 minute.
3. Pour your spaghetti egg mixture into your skillet and sprinkle with your bacon pieces. Add your mozzarella, tomatoes, basil, and olives on top. Lower your heat and allow to cook for 3 minutes until the eggs have set on the bottom. Transfer your pan into the oven and cook for approximately 15 to 20 minutes. Remove from the oven and let it cool before serving.

NUTRITION: Calories 55 Fats 21g Fiber 4g Carbohydrate 7g Protein 32g

16. Hearty Breakfast Frittata With Tomato Salad

Preparation Time: 25 minutes

Cooking Time: 15 minutes

Servings: 4

INGREDIENTS:

- 4 Eggs

- 1 tablespoon of Vegetable Oil
- 1 2 3 pounds of Sliced and Peeled Potatoes
- 2 Onions (1 Diced 1 Sliced into Rings)
- 1 Small Diced Zucchini
- 1 ounce of Pitted and Sliced Black Olives
- 5 1 4 ounces of Diced Salami
- 12 ounces of Diced Tomatoes
- 1 third cup of Whipping Cream
- 5 sprigs of Sliced Basil
- 1 teaspoon of Balsamic Vinegar
- 2 tablespoons of Olive Oil

DIRECTIONS:

1. Heat your vegetable oil in a pan and fry your potatoes for approximately 12 minutes.
2. Add your onion rings, zucchini, olives, and salami. Sauté for another 5 minutes.
3. Beat your cream and eggs together. Season them and pour over the vegetables. Cover and cook over a medium heat for approximately 10 minutes.
4. Toss together your diced onions, diced tomatoes, vinegar, olive oil, and basil. Season to taste. Slice your frittata into quarters and arrange with your tomato salad on plates.

NUTRITION: Calories 65 Fats 11g Fiber 4g Carbohydrate 7g Protein 32g

17. Breakfast Quesadilla

Preparation Time: 15 minutes

Cooking Time: 15 minutes

Servings: 2

INGREDIENTS:

- 1 Skinless Boneless Chicken Breast
- 2 Large Eggs
- 2 Egg Whites
- 1 cup of Chopped Baby Spinach
- 1 tablespoon of Extra-Virgin Olive Oil
- 1 half cup of Chopped Tomatoes
- 1 fourth cup of Sour Cream
- 2 third cup of Shredded Cheddar and Jack Cheese Blend
- 1 Pitted and Chopped Avocado
- 1 fourth cup of Sliced Black Olives
- 3 Sliced Green Onions
- 2 tablespoons of Chopped Fresh Cilantro
- Salsa
- Tortillas

DIRECTIONS:

1. Preheat your broiler.
2. Pound your chicken breast lightly using a meat pounder.
3. Season with pepper and salt. Broil on your broiler pan for approximately 4 to 5 minutes on each side. Cook until the chicken is done and no longer pink on the inside.
4. Transfer to your chopping board and dice the chicken breast.

1. Quesadilla:

1. Preheat your oven to 200 degrees.
2. In a bowl, whisk your eggs together.
3. Heat your oil in a frying pan over a medium heat.
4. Add your egg mixture to your pan and cook until the edges have begun to set.
5. Stir with your spatula, scraping eggs on the bottom and sides of your pan and fold them toward the center.
6. Add your spinach, chicken, and tomatoes. Continue to cook.
7. Stir frequently until your eggs are fluffy and light. Remove your pan from heat and set to the side.
8. Drizzle olive oil on a separate frying pan over a medium heat. Place a tortilla in a pan and heat up until it is warmed.
9. Flip your tortilla and sprinkle the bottom half with 1 third cup of your cheese mixture.
10. Top your cheese with half of your egg mixture.
11. Fold your tortilla in half in your pan to cover the eggs and cheese.
12. Cook until golden brown on the bottom of tortilla.
13. Flip your quesadilla and cook the opposite side until golden brown.
14. Transfer to your baking sheet to keep it warm while cooking your second quesadilla.
15. Cut each into wedges. Top with cilantro, sour cream, avocado, olives, green onions, and salsa.

NUTRITION: Calories 75 Fats 21g Fiber 7g Carbohydrate 17g Protein 32g

18. Roquefort Pear Toast

Preparation Time: 20 minutes

Cooking Time: 15 minutes

Servings: 3

INGREDIENTS:

- 8 slices of walnut bread (120 g)
- 1 jar of 100 g of white cheese with 3% fat
- 60 g of Roquefort cheese
- 2 ripe Williams or Guyot pears
- 1 lemon
- 4 nuts

DIRECTION:

1. Toast the slices of bread.
2. Remove the nuts from their shells.
3. Mix together the cottage cheese and Roquefort cheese. Spread toast with this mixture.

4. Wash the lemon, sponge it, and squeeze its juice.
5. Wash the pears, peel them, remove their central part and their pips, divide them into tiny dice. Lemon immediately to prevent the pears from turning black.
6. Spread the pears over the toasts. Add a walnut kernel per toast.

NUTRITION: Calories 55 Fats 21g Fiber 4g Carbohydrate 7g Protein 32g

19. Chickpea Salad

Preparation Time: 20 minutes

Cooking Time: 15 minutes

Servings: 3

INGREDIENTS:

- 150 g chickpeas
- 1 onion
- 1 clove
- 1 clove of garlic
- 1 bouquet garni
- 200 g celery-branch
- 1 lemon
- 5 tablespoons of olive oil
- 1 tip of curry
- 1 tablespoon chopped chives
- Salt pepper

DIRECTIONS:

1. Position the chickpeas in a large bowl filled with cold water and let them soak for 12 hours.
2. Peel the onion and garlic. Drain the chickpeas. Place them in a casserole with 1 2 liters of cold water, the bouquet garni, and the onion stuck clove, the clove of garlic, some grains of pepper. Cover, cook for 2 hours.
3. Wash the celery, detach its branches from the bulb, remove the top of the leaves, detail it in the sticks.
4. Wash the lemon and squeeze its juice — mix 2 tablespoons with the olive oil and the curry.
5. Drain the chickpeas well. Mix with celery. Add salt and pepper. Season with the olive oil vinaigrette and add the chives.

NUTRITION: Calories 45 Fats 11g Fiber 4g Carbohydrate 7g Protein 32g

20. Hot Shrimp Avocado Salad

Preparation Time: 15 minutes

Cooking Time: 10-15 minutes

Servings: 4-6

INGREDIENTS:

- 1 tablespoon butter

- 11 2 teaspoons curry powder
- 11 4 teaspoons salt
- 1 medium tomato, chopped
- 1 medium onion, chopped 11 2 pounds fresh shrimp, cleaned and well-drained
- 2 tablespoons lemon juice
- 1 1 4 cup sour cream
- 3 or 4 avocados, peeled

DIRECTIONS:

1. Melt butter and stir in curry powder and salt. Add tomato, onion, and shrimp, and sauté until shrimp are done, and seasoning is soft. Add lemon juice. If the mixture is a bit watery, drain some of the liquid at this point. Stir in sour cream and heat thoroughly. Serve hot as follows:
2. For a salad meal, halve avocados and scoop in shrimp mixture. For a salad accompaniment, spoon onto lettuce and surround with slices of avocado.

NUTRITION: Calories 134 Fats 3g Fiber 13g Carbohydrate 23g Protein 2g

21. <u>Middle East Rice Salad</u>

Preparation Time: 10 minutes

Cooking Time: 12 minutes

Servings: 4

INGREDIENTS:

- 2 tablespoons of olive oil
- 1 2 Vidalia or other sweet onion, in thin slices (about 3 4 cup)
- 1 can (16 ounces) chickpeas, rinsed and drained
- 1 2 teaspoon ground cumin
- 1 fourth teaspoon of salt
- Freshly ground black pepper
- 3 cups cooked brown rice
- 1 2 cup chopped dates
- 1 4 cup minced fresh mint
- 1 fourth cup of chopped fresh parsley

DIRECTIONS:

1. Heat the oil in a large nonstick skillet over medium-high heat.
2. Add the onion and cook, frequently stirring, about 5 minutes or until the onion begins to brown. Remove from heat and add the chickpeas, cumin, and salt.
3. Season to taste with freshly ground black pepper.
4. In a large bowl, combine rice, onion and chickpea mixture, dates, mint, and parsley.
5. Mix well until completely combined.
6. Serve hot or at room temperature.

NUTRITION: Calories 127 Fat 6g Carbohydrates 11.6g Sugar 7g Protein 6.8g Cholesterol 16 mg

22. Sardou Eggs

Preparation Time: 20 minutes

Cooking Time: 35 minutes

Servings: 4

INGREDIENTS:

- 3 large egg yolks, at room temperature
- 1 tablespoon tomato paste
- 1 tablespoon lemon juice
- 1 tablespoon cool water
- 1 teaspoon hot sauce
- 1 teaspoon Worcestershire sauce
- ½ teaspoon salt
- ½ teaspoon cayenne pepper
- ½ cup (1 stick) unsalted butter, melted Creamed Spinach:
- ½ tablespoon olive oil
- ½ cup minced onion
- 1-pound frozen chopped spinach
- 1 (8-ounce) package cream cheese, softened
- 1 4 cup shredded Parmesan cheese
- Kosher salt
- Ground white pepper
- 1 tablespoon unsalted butter
- 16 canned artichoke heart quarters
- 1 (2-ounce) can anchovies, drained and chopped (optional)
- 1 teaspoon paprika
- Large poached eggs

DIRECTIONS:

1. To make the choron sauce: In a large stainless-steel bowl set over a pot of simmering water combine the egg yolks, tomato paste, lemon juice, water, hot sauce, Worcestershire sauce, salt, and cayenne pepper. Whisk nonstop until the mixture is a pale light-yellow color, the volume increases to almost double, and, when the whisk is put up away from the sauce, it's thick enough to drip back into the bowl in a ribbon.

2. 2 Take the bowl out from the hot water bath, place it on the counter, and, while continuing to whisk, add the butter in a slow, steady stream. Start with just a few drops of the butter first, then gradually increase the amount. Add it slowly, and you'll get a beautiful, thick emulsion; add it too quickly, and the sauce will break, or separate. If the Hollandaise seems too thick, gradually whisk in a bit of water to thin it out. Set the sauce aside in the bowl at room temperature (if you try to reheat choron sauce, it will break).

3. 3 To make the creamed spinach: Heat the oil in a medium saucepan over medium heat and sauté the onion for about 5 minutes, until translucent. Add the spinach and cream cheese. Mix well over low heat

and cook for about 3 minutes, until well blended. Put Parmesan cheese and season Keep covered over low heat.

4. 4 To assemble the Eggs Sardou: Melt the butter in a small skillet over medium heat and cook the artichoke hearts for about 2 minutes, turning once, until heated through.

5. 5 Divide the creamed spinach among 4 warm plates. Arrange 4 artichoke heart quarters around the spinach on each plate. Sprinkle the spinach with the anchovies (if using). Put poached eggs on top, drizzle with 2 tablespoons of choron sauce, and sprinkle with 1 fourth teaspoon of paprika. Serve immediately.

NUTRITION: Calories 224 Fat 19.1g Fiber 6.4g Carbohydrate 21.5g Protein 3.5.g

23. Tomato Zoodle Salad

Preparation time: 10 minutes

Cooking time: 0 minutes

Servings: 2

INGREDIENTS:

- Zucchinis, cut with a spiralizer- 2
- Olive oil- 1 tbsp
- Salt and black pepper- to taste
- Mozzarella, shredded- ½ cup
- Cherry tomatoes, halved- 1 cup
- Basil, torn- 2 tbsp
- Balsamic vinegar - 1 tbsp

DIRECTIONS:

1. Toss zucchini noodles (zoodles) with oil, salt, and pepper in a suitable bowl.
2. Let these noodles sit for 10 minutes at room temperature then stir in tomatoes, basil, vinegar, and mozzarella.
3. Serve fresh.

NUTRITION: Calories 318 Fat 14g Fiber 5g Carbohydrate 29g Protein 11 g

24. Dill Topped Squash And Cucumber Mix

Preparation Time: 30 minutes

Cooking time: 30 minutes

Servings: 4

INGREDIENTS:

- Yellow summer squash: sliced – 1
- Cherry tomatoes: halved- 1 cup
- Minced garlic clove- 1
- Chopped dill- 1 tbsp.
- Cucumber: sliced- 1
- 1 third cup of cider vinegar
- Stevia- 2 tsp.
- Salt
- Black pepper

DIRECTIONS:

1. Mix squash, cucumber, tomatoes, stevia, salt, pepper, garlic, and vinegar in a bowl.
2. Cover and let it chill in the fridge for 30 minutes.
3. Flip with the chopped dill.
4. Serve.

NUTRITION: Calories 130 Carbohydrate 5g Protein 8g Fiber 2g Fat 10 g

25. Seasoned Okra With Tomatoes

Preparation Time: 10 minutes

Cooking Time: 15 minutes

Servings: 6

INGREDIENTS:

- Okra pods: quartered- 15
- Sliced tomatoes- 3
- Crushed red pepper- ½ tsp.
- Grated parmesan- 1 4 cup
- Chopped tarragon- 2 tsp.
- Chopped scallion- 1
- Coconut cream- 1 4 cup
- Avocado mayonnaise- 1 4 cup
- Almond milk- 3 tbsp.
- Sliced red onion- 1
- Olive oil- 3 tbsp.
- Lemon juice- 2 tsp.

- Grated lemon zest- 1 tsp.
- Salt and black pepper

DIRECTIONS:

1. Combine okra, a pinch of salt, pepper, 2 tbsp. of olive oil together in a bowl and spread on a lined baking sheet.
2. Bake in the oven for 15 minutes at 4000F.
3. Pour the remaining oil into the pan over medium-high and fry the onion for 3 minutes, remove and set aside.
4. Mix tomatoes with the fried onions together with red pepper, roasted okra and salt, and pepper.
5. Combine coconut cream, almond milk, tarragon, mayonnaise, Parmesan, scallions, onion, zest and juice and mix well in a bowl.
6. Add the cream mix to the okra and tomatoes mix and serve.

NUTRITION Calories 137 Carbohydrate 7g Protein 3g Fiber 2g Fats 12 g

26. Savory Celery Stir-Fry

Preparation Time: 10 minutes

Cooking Time: 5 minutes

Servings: 6

INGREDIENTS:

- Celery: julienned- 4 cups
- Chili peppers: dried and crushed- 3
- Coconut aminos- 2 tbsp.
- Olive oil- 2 tbsp.

DIRECTIONS:

1. Pour oil on a pan over medium-high and add the peppers to cook for 2 minutes.
2. Stir in the coconut aminos and the celery and let it cook for 3 minutes.
3. Serve.

NUTRITION Calories 61 Carbohydrate 4g Protein 1g Fiber 1g Fats 5 g

27. Easy Celery And Squash Jumble

Preparation Time: 15 minutes

Cooking Time: 7 minutes

Servings: 2

INGREDIENTS:

- Chopped celery- 4 oz.
- Veggie stock- 2 cups
- Squash: seeded and chopped roughly- 7 oz.
- Salt and black pepper

DIRECTIONS:

1. Pour the veggie stock in a pot and let simmer over medium heat.
2. Add the celery, salt, pepper, squash and let it cook for 12 minutes.
3. Remove the liquid and serve.

NUTRITION Calories 85 Carbohydrate 10g Protein 3g Fiber 4g Fats 15 g

28. Creamy Polenta

Preparation Time: 8 minutes

Cooking Time: forty-five minutes

Servings: 4

INGREDIENTS:

½ cup cream

1 ½ cup water

1 cup polenta

1 3 cup Parmesan, grated

2 cups chicken stock

DIRECTIONS:

1. Put polenta in the pot.
2. Put in water, chicken stock, cream, and Parmesan. Mix up polenta well.
3. Then preheat oven to 355F.
4. Cook polenta in your oven for about forty-five minutes.
5. Mix up the cooked meal with the help of the spoon cautiously before you serve.

NUTRITION: Calories 208 Fat 5.3g Fiber 1g Carbohydrate 32.2gProtein 8 g

29. Crispy Corn

Preparation Time: 8 minutes

Cooking Time: five minutes

Servings: 3

INGREDIENTS:

- ½ teaspoon ground paprika
- ½ teaspoon salt
- ¾ teaspoon chili pepper
- 1 cup corn kernels
- 1 tablespoon coconut flour
- 1 tablespoon water
- 3 tablespoons canola oil

DIRECTIONS:

1. In the mixing container, mix together corn kernels with salt and coconut flour.
2. Put in water and mix up the corn with the help of the spoon.
3. Pour canola oil in the frying pan and heat it.

4. Put in corn kernels mixture and roast it for about four minutes. Stir it occasionally.
5. When the corn kernels are crispy, move them in the plate and dry with the paper towels help.
6. Put in chili pepper and ground paprika. Mix up well.

Nutrition: Calories 179Fat 15g Fiber 2.4gCarbohydrate 11.3g Protein 2.1 g

30. Cucumber Yogurt Salad With Mint

Preparation Time: ten minutes

Cooking Time: 0 minutes

Servings: 2

INGREDIENTS:

- 1 4 cup organic coconut milk
- 1 4 cup organic mint leaves
- 1 4 teaspoon pink Himalayan sea salt
- ½ cup chopped organic red onion
- 1 tablespoon virgin olive oil
- 1 tablespoon plain organic goat yogurt
- 1 teaspoon organic dill weed
- 2 chopped organic cucumbers
- 3 tablespoons fresh organic lime juice

DIRECTIONS:

1. Cut the red onion, dill, cucumbers, and mint and mix them in a big container.
2. Blend them until they're smooth.
3. Top the dressing onto the cucumber salad and mix meticulously. Chill for minimum 1 hour and serve.
4. Enjoy!

NUTRITION: Calories 207 Protein 6.9g Fat: 13.87 gCarbohydrates: 18.04 g

31. Curry Wheatberry Rice

Preparation Time: ten minutes

Cooking Time: 1 hour fifteen minutes

Servings: 5

INGREDIENTS:

- 1 4 cup milk
- ½ cup of rice
- 1 cup wheat berries
- 1 tablespoon curry paste
- 1 teaspoon salt
- 4 tablespoons olive oil
- 6 cups chicken stock

DIRECTIONS:

1. Put wheatberries and chicken stock in the pan.
2. Close the lid and cook the mixture for an hour over the moderate heat.
3. Then put in rice, olive oil, and salt.
4. Stir thoroughly.
5. Mix up together milk and curry paste.
6. Put in the curry liquid in the rice-wheatberry mixture and stir thoroughly.
7. Boil the meal for fifteen minutes with the closed lid.
8. When the rice is cooked, all the meal is cooked.

NUTRITION: Calories 232 Fat 15g Fiber 1.4g Carbohydrate 23.5g Protein: 3.9 g

32. Couscous Salad

Preparation Time: ten minutes

Cooking Time: six minutes

Servings: 4

INGREDIENTS:

- 1 4 teaspoon ground black pepper
- ¾ teaspoon ground coriander
- ½ teaspoon salt
- 1 fourth teaspoon paprika
- 1 fourth teaspoon turmeric
- 1 tablespoon butter
- 2 oz. chickpeas, canned, drained
- 1 cup fresh arugula, chopped
- 2 oz. sun-dried tomatoes, chopped
- 1 oz. Feta cheese, crumbled
- 1 tablespoon canola oil
- 1 3 cup couscous
- 1 3 cup chicken stock

DIRECTIONS:

1. Bring the chicken stock to boil.
2. Put in couscous, ground black pepper, ground coriander, salt, paprika, and turmeric. Put in chickpeas and butter. Mix the mixture well and close the lid.
3. Allow the couscous soak the hot chicken stock for about six minutes.
4. In the meantime, in the mixing container mix together arugula, sun-dried tomatoes, and Feta cheese.
5. Put in cooked couscous mixture and canola oil.
6. Mix up the salad well.

NUTRITION: Calories 18 Fat: 9g Fiber: 3.6g Carbs: 21.1g Protein: 6 g

33. Cool Garbanzo And Spinach Beans

Preparation Time: 5-ten minutes

Cooking Time: 0 minute

Servings: 4

INGREDIENTS:

- ½ onion, diced
- ½ teaspoon cumin
- 1 tablespoon olive oil
- 10 ounces spinach, chopped
- 12 ounces garbanzo beans

DIRECTIONS:

1. Take a frying pan and put in olive oil
2. Put it on moderate to low heat
3. Put in onions, garbanzo and cook for five minutes
4. Mix in cumin, garbanzo beans, spinach and flavor with sunflower seeds
5. Use a spoon to smash gently
6. Cook meticulously
7. Serve and enjoy!

NUTRITION: Calories: 90 Fat: 4g Carbohydrates: 11g Protein:4g

34. Citrus Couscous With Herb

Preparation Time: five minutes

Cooking Time: fifteen minutes

Servings: 2

INGREDIENTS:

- 1 fourth cup of water
- 1 fourth orange, chopped
- ½ teaspoon butter
- 1 teaspoon Italian seasonings
- 1 3 cup couscous
- 1 3 teaspoon salt
- 4 tablespoons orange juice

DIRECTIONS:

1. Pour water and orange juice in the pan.
2. Put in orange, Italian seasoning, and salt.
3. Bring the liquid to boil and take it off the heat.
4. Put in butter and couscous. Stir thoroughly and close the lid.
5. Leave the couscous rest for about ten minutes.

NUTRITION: Calories 149 Fat: 1.9g Fiber: 2.1g Carbs: 28.5g Protein: 4.1 g

35. Cilantro And Avocado Platter

Preparation Time: ten minutes

Cooking Time: 0 minutes

Servings: 6

INGREDIENTS:

- 1 fourth cup of fresh cilantro, chopped
- ½ a lime, juiced
- 1 big ripe tomato, chopped
- 1 green bell pepper, chopped
- 1 sweet onion, chopped
- 2 avocados, peeled, pitted and diced
- Salt and pepper as required

DIRECTIONS:

1. Take a moderate-sized container and put in onion, bell pepper, tomato, avocados, lime and cilantro
2. Mix thoroughly and give it a toss
3. Sprinkle with salt and pepper in accordance with your taste
4. Serve and enjoy!

NUTRITION: Calories: 126 Fat: 10g Carbohydrates: 10g Protein: 2g

36. Cauliflower Broccoli Mash

Preparation Time: five minutes

Cooking Time: ten minutes

Servings: 6

INGREDIENTS:

- 1 big head cauliflower, cut into chunks
- 1 small head broccoli, cut into florets
- 1 teaspoon salt
- 3 tablespoons extra virgin olive oil
- Pepper, to taste

DIRECTIONS:

1. Take a pot and put in oil then heat it
2. Put in the cauliflower and broccoli
3. Sprinkle with salt and pepper to taste
4. Keep stirring to make vegetable soft
5. Put in water if required
6. When is already cooked, use a food processor or a potato masher to puree the vegetables?
7. Serve and enjoy!

NUTRITION: Calories: 39 Fat: 3g Carbohydrates: 2g Protein: 0.89g

37. Caramelized Pears And Onions

Preparation Time: five minutes

Cooking Time: thirty-five minutes

Servings: 4

INGREDIENTS:

- 1 tablespoon olive oil
- 2 firm red pears, cored and quartered
- 2 red onion, cut into wedges
- Salt and pepper, to taste

DIRECTIONS:

1. Preheat the oven to 425 degrees F
2. Put the pears and onion on a baking tray
3. Sprinkle with olive oil
4. Sprinkle with salt and pepper
5. Bake using your oven for a little more than half an hour
6. Serve and enjoy!

NUTRITION: Calories: 101 Fat: 4g Carbohydrates: 17g Protein: 1g

38. Parsnips With Tahini Dressing

Preparation Time: 10 minutes

Cooking Time: 10 minutes

Servings: 4

INGREDIENTS:

- For Parsnips
- 1 teaspoon olive oil
- ½ teaspoon salt
- 3 large parsnips, peeled, halved lengthwise, and cut into 1" half-moons
- For Tahini Dressing
- 1 tablespoon tahini
- 1 tablespoon fresh lemon juice
- 1 teaspoon water
- 1 clove garlic, peeled and minced
- 1 tablespoon chopped fresh parsley

DIRECTIONS:

1. To make Parsnips: Preheat air fryer at 375°F for 3 minutes.
2. In a medium bowl, whisk together olive oil and salt. Add parsnips and toss.

3. Add parsnips to ungreased air fryer basket and cook 5 minutes. Toss, then cook an additional 5 minutes.
4. To make Tahini Dressing: While parsnips are cooking, whisk together tahini, lemon juice, water, and garlic in a medium bowl.
5. Add cooked parsnips and toss. Transfer to a medium serving dish. Garnish with parsley. Serve.

NUTRITION: Calories: 82 Protein: 2g Fiber: 3g Net Carbohydrates: 9g Fat: 3g Sodium: 299mg
Carbohydrates: 13g

39. Seasoned Green Beans

Preparation Time: 5 minutes

Cooking Time: 10 minutes

Servings: 4

INGREDIENTS:

- 2 cups fresh green beans, ends trimmed
- 1 tablespoon butter, melted
- ½ teaspoon salt
- 1 fourth teaspoon freshly ground black pepper
- 1 slice sugar-free bacon, diced
- 1 clove garlic, peeled and minced
- 1 lemon wedge

DIRECTIONS:

1. Preheat air fryer at 375°F for 3 minutes.
2. In a medium bowl, toss together green beans, butter, salt, and pepper.
3. Add green beans to ungreased air fryer basket and cook 5 minutes. Toss in bacon and cook an additional 4 minutes. Toss in minced garlic and cook an additional minute.
4. Transfer to a medium serving dish, squeeze lemon over beans, and toss. Serve warm.

NUTRITION: Calories: 51 Protein: 2g Fiber: 1g Net Carbohydrates: 3g Fat: 4g Sodium: 331mg
Carbohydrates: 4g Sugar: 2g

40. Baked Garlic Ricotta

Preparation Time: 10 minutes

Cooking Time: 7 minutes

Servings: 4

INGREDIENTS:

- 2 cloves peeled Simple Roasted Garlic
- 1½ cups ricotta cheese
- ½ cup grated Parmesan cheese
- 1 large egg, beaten
- 1 tablespoon olive oil

- 1 tablespoon fresh lemon juice
- 1 4 teaspoon salt
- 1 fourth teaspoon freshly ground black pepper
- 1 teaspoon finely chopped fresh rosemary

DIRECTIONS:

1. Preheat air fryer to 350°F for 3 minutes.
2. Squeeze garlic into a medium bowl. Using the back of a fork, mash until a garlic paste is formed. Add remaining ingredients and combine.
3. Spoon mixture into an ungreased 6" oven-safe baking dish.
4. Place dishes in air fryer basket. Cook 7 minutes.
5. Serve warm.

NUTRITION: Calories: 257 Protein: 16g Fiber: 0g Net Carbohydrates: 5g Fat: 16g Sodium: 411mg Carbohydrates: 5g Sugar: 1g

41. Whiting Bread With Sesame

Preparation Time: 10 minutes

Cooking Time: 10 minutes

INGREDIENTS:

- 400 g whiting fillets
- 4 tablespoons sesame oil
- 1 lemon
- 1 tablespoon soy sauce
- 1 clove of garlic
- 2 tablespoons minced lemongrass
- 1 small piece of ginger 1 cm
- 4 tablespoons sesame seeds
- 2 eggs
- Salt pepper

DIRECTION:

1. Wash the lemon under running water, sponge it, squeeze it. Peel and slice the clove of garlic. Pass the ginger under the water, sponge it, grate it.
2. Prepare a marinade with 2 tablespoons of sesame oil, lemon juice, soy sauce, lemongrass, garlic, ginger, and a little pepper. Arrange the whiting fillets in the marinade and reserve them in the refrigerator for 2 hours.
3. Then very carefully drain the fish fillets. Cook them for 5 minutes, steaming.
4. Separate the egg whites from the yolks. Spread each fillet of whiting in the egg yolk and then in the sesame seeds to form a breadcrumb. Salt slightly. Quickly pass the breaded fish fillets in a non-stick frying pan with the remaining 2 spoons of oil. As soon as the sesame seeds are golden brown, stop cooking. Enjoy it immediately.

NUTRITION: Calories: 257 Protein: 16g Fiber: 0g Net Carbohydrates: 5g Fat: 16g Sodium: 411mg

Carbohydrates: 5 Sugar: 1g

42. Crab Montage With Mushroom Soup

Preparation Time: 20 minutes

Cooking Time: 15-20 minutes

Servings: 6-8

INGREDIENTS:

- 1 can cream of mushroom soup
- 1 can crab meat, drained
- 1 bunch green onions, chopped
- 2 (8-ounce) package cream cheese
- 1 cup chopped celery
- 1 2 red bell pepper, chopped
- 2 envelopes gelatin
- 1 tablespoon lemon juice
- 1 4 cup water
- 1 cup mayonnaise
- 2 cans shrimp, drained
- Hot sauce to taste

DIRECTIONS:

1. Heat soup. Dissolve cream cheese in the soup. Dissolve gelatin in cold water. Add to soup. Add remaining ingredients. Place in a mold and refrigerate. Serve with crackers.

NUTRITION: Calories 115 Fat: 1.8g Fiber: 2.1gg Carbs: 12.9g Protein: 3g

Spicy Tomato Salad

Preparation Time: 2 hrs.

Cooking Time: 0 minutes

Servings: 8

INGREDIENTS:

- 4 yellow banana peppers, seeded and diced
- 2 green banana peppers, seeded and diced
- 2 jalapeno peppers, seeded and diced
- 5 large tomatoes, seeded and diced
- 2 garlic cloves, minced
- 1 tbs. chopped fresh basil
- 1 tbs. chopped fresh parsley
- 1 tsp. chopped fresh rosemary
- 1 tsp. chopped fresh oregano
- 2 oz. cheddar cheese, cubed

- 1 2 cup olive oil
- 1 tbs. fresh lemon juice
- 1 tsp. salt
- 1 2 tsp. black pepper

DIRECTIONS:

2. In a serving bowl, add the green and yellow banana peppers, jalapeno peppers, tomatoes, garlic, basil, parsley, rosemary, oregano and cheddar cheese. In a jar that comes with a lid, put olive oil, lemon juice, salt and black pepper. Cover the jar and shake until all the ingredients are combined. Pour the dressing over the peppers and tomatoes. Toss until all the ingredients are combined.
3. Cover the bowl and chill at least 2 hours but not more than 4 hours. Drain all the liquid from the salad and serve.

Nutrition: Calories 129 Fat: 2.3g Fiber: 3.1g Carbs: 10.4g Protein: 2.5g

43. _Number 0Baked Sole With Cauliflower Salad_

Preparation Time: 15-20 minutes

Cooking Time: 50 minutes

Servings: 8

INGREDIENTS:

- 8 sole fillets
- 3 C. French style green beans
- 3 C. cauliflower, florets
- 1 tbsp butter
- 1 8 C. lemon juice
- 1 green onion
- salt
- pepper
- Cajun seasoning

DIRECTIONS:

1. The oven must heat to 450F.
2. Place the sole fillets on a greased baking pan. Drizzle over them the fresh lemon juice followed by the Cajun seasoning.
3. Place the sole sheet in the oven and let it cool for 32 min
4. Place the cauliflower in a heatproof bowl. Cook it in the microwave for 9 min.
5. Get a heatproof bowl: Stir in it the green beans with green onion. Cook them in the microwave for 9 min.
6. Drain the coked veggies. Add to them the butter with a pinch of salt and pepper. Toss them to coat.
7. Serve your baked sole with the veggie salad.
8. Enjoy.

NUTRITION: Calories 280 Fat: 10.6h Fiber: 12.5g Carbs: 28g Protein: 15.1g

44. Tasty Fish Curry

Preparation Time: 10 minutes

Cooking Time: 7 minutes

Servings: 4

INGREDIENTS:

- Boneless cod fillets, 4
- Chopped yellow onion, 1
- Canned tomatoes, 12 oz.
- Olive oil, 1 tbsp.
- Veggie stock, 7 oz.
- Curry paste, 2 tbsps.
- Minced garlic clove, 1

DIRECTIONS:

1. Set up the pot with oil on the fire to cook the onion for 3 minutes over medium-high heat
2. Mix in the tomatoes, curry paste, garlic, cod fillets, and stock.
3. Allow to simmer for 10 minutes while covered
4. Divide among plates and enjoys

NUTRITION Calories: 164, Fat: 8gFiber: 4g Net Carbs: 3gProtein: 22 g

45. Easy Cod

Preparation Time: 10 minutes

Cooking Time: 10 minutes

Servings: 4

INGREDIENTS:

- Cooking spray
- Chicken stock, 1 4 c.
- Minced garlic cloves, 2
- Salt
- Basil, 1 4 c.
- Black pepper
- Skinless cod fillets, 4
- Olive oil, 4 tsps.

DIRECTIONS:

1. Set your blender in position then add garlic, basil, pepper, stock, salt, and oil to process until done
2. Set the mixture in a bowl then combine with the fish to coat well
3. Spray the pan then add the fish to cook evenly, for about 5minutes
4. Set on plates the serve with salad as a side dish.

NUTRITION Calories: 128, Fat: 8g Fiber: 1gNet Carbs: 0.3g Protein: 18 g

46. Pan-Fried Cod With Saffron

Preparation Time: 10 minutes

Cooking Time: 10 minutes

Servings: 4

INGREDIENTS:

- Boneless cod fillets, 4
- Olive oil, 2 tbsps.
- Chopped chili pepper, 1 tsp.
- Veggie stock, 1 4 c.
- Chopped canned tomatoes, 14 oz.
- Bay leaves, 2
- Minced garlic cloves, 2
- Saffron powder

DIRECTIONS:

1. Set your pan on fire to with oil to cook garlic and chili pepper for 3 minutes over medium heat
2. Stir in the bay leaves, tomatoes, saffron, and stock to cook for seven minutes
3. Mix in the fish, adjust the seasoning and cook for seven minutes while covers
4. Remove the bay leaves, set on plates and enjoy

NUTRITION Calories: 151Fat: 9gFiber: 1gNet Carbs: 2gProtein: 20g

47. Rosemary Flounder

Preparation Time: 10 minutes

Cooking Time: 10 minutes

Servings: 2

INGREDIENTS:

- Chopped rosemary springs, 3
- Olive oil, 1 tbsp.
- Salt
- Flounder fillets, 2
- Black pepper
- Minced garlic cloves, 3
- Lemon wedges for serving

DIRECTIONS:

1. Set the pan on fire heat with oil for frying rosemary, pepper, garlic, and salt for 4 minutes over medium-high heat
2. Cook the fish in the mixture until done on both sides.
3. Set on plates with lemon wedges
4. Enjoy

NUTRITION Calories: 192, Fat: 15gFiber: 4gNet Carbs: 5g Protein: 12 g

48. Stuffed Oysters

Preparation Time: 15 minutes

Cooking Time: 15 minutes

Servings: 3

INGREDIENTS:

- Cooked and chopped slices bacon, 2
- Chopped parsley, 1tsp.
- Mustard, ½ tsp.
- Black pepper
- Melted ghee, 1 tbsp.
- Shucked big oysters top, 6
- Salt

DIRECTIONS:

1. Set the mixing bowl in place to whisk together ghee, parsley, pepper, mustard, and salt
2. Top one teaspoon of this mixture on each oyster followed by chopped bacon.
3. Set the oyster fillets in a baking sheet

4. Set the oven for 10 minutes at 4500F, allow to bake
5. Serve on plates and enjoy

NUTRITION Calories: 43, Fat: 5gFiber: 1g Net Carbs: 0.5g Protein: 3 g

49. Seared Sea Scallops

Preparation Time: 5 minutes

Cooking Time: 8 minutes

Servings: 2

INGREDIENTS:

- 2 tablespoons butter, melted
- 1 tablespoon fresh lemon juice
- 1-pound (about 10) jumbo sea scallops

DIRECTIONS:

1. Preheat air fryer at 400°F for 3 minutes.
2. In a small bowl, combine butter and lemon juice. Roll scallops in mixture to coat all sides.
3. Place scallops in ungreased air fryer basket. Cook 2 minutes.
4. Flip scallops. Cook 2 minutes more.
5. Brush the tops of each scallop with butter mixture. Cook 2 minutes. Flip scallops. Cook an additional 2 minutes.
6. Transfer scallops to a large serving plate and serve warm.

NUTRITION: Calories: 260 Protein: 27g Fiber: 0g Net carbohydrates: 8g Fat: 13g Sodium: 891mg

Carbohydrates: 8g Sugar: 0g

50. Salmon Cakes With Lemon Caper Sauce

Preparation Time: 10 minutes

Cooking Time: 20 minutes

Servings: 4

INGREDIENTS:

- For Lemon Caper Sauce
- 1 4 cup sour cream
- 2 tablespoons mayonnaise
- 2 cloves garlic, peeled and minced
- 1 4 teaspoon caper juice
- 2 teaspoons lemon juice
- For Salmon Patties
- 1 (14.75-ounce) can salmon, drained
- ½ cup mayonnaise
- 2 teaspoons lemon zest

- 1 large egg
- 2 tablespoons seeded and finely minced red bell pepper
- ½ cup almond meal
- 1 8 teaspoon salt
- 2 tablespoons capers, drained

DIRECTIONS:

1. To make Lemon Caper Sauce: In a small bowl, combine sour cream, mayonnaise, garlic, caper juice, and lemon juice. Refrigerate covered until ready to use.
2. To make Salmon Patties: Preheat air fryer at 400°F for 3 minutes.
3. In a medium bowl, combine salmon, mayonnaise, lemon zest, egg, bell pepper, almond meal, and salt. Form into eight patties.
4. Place four patties in air fryer basket lightly greased with olive oil. Cook 5 minutes. Gently flip and cook an additional 5 minutes.
5. Transfer cooked patties to a large serving dish and repeat cooking with remaining patties. Let rest 5 minutes, then drizzle with lemon caper sauce and garnish with capers. Serve.

NUTRITION: Calories: 471 Protein: 21g Fiber: 2g Net carbohydrates: 3g Fat: 41g Sodium: 832mg Carbohydrates: 5g Sugar: 1g

51. Classic Lobster Salad

Preparation Time: 10 minutes

Cooking Time: 8 minutes

Servings: 2

INGREDIENTS:

1. 2 (6-ounce) uncooked lobster tails, thawed
2. 1 4 cup mayonnaise
3. 2 teaspoons fresh lemon juice
4. 1 small stalk celery, sliced
5. 2 teaspoons chopped fresh chives
6. 2 teaspoons chopped fresh tarragon
7. 1 4 teaspoon salt
8. 1 8 teaspoons freshly ground black pepper
9. 2 thick slices large beefsteak tomato
10. 1 small avocado, peeled, pitted, and diced

DIRECTIONS:

1. Preheat air fryer at 400°F for 3 minutes.
2. Using kitchen shears, cut down the middle of each lobster tail on the softer side. Carefully run your finger between the lobster meat and the shell to loosen meat.
3. Place lobster tails cut sides up, in ungreased air fryer basket. Cook 8 minutes.
4. Transfer tails to a large plate and let cool about 3 minutes until easy to handle, then pull lobster meat from shell. Roughly chop meat and add to a medium bowl.
5. Add mayonnaise, lemon juice, celery, chives, tarragon, salt, and pepper to bowl. Combine.

6. Divide lobster salad between two medium plates, top with tomato slices, and garnish with avocado. Serve.

NUTRITION: Calories: 463 Protein: 24g Fiber: 7g Net carbohydrates: 5g Fat: 36g Sodium: 1,343mg Carbohydrates: 12g Sugar: 3g

52. Buttery Lobster Tails

Preparation Time: 10 minutes

Cooking Time: 8 minutes

Servings: 2

INGREDIENTS:

- 2 (6-ounce) uncooked lobster tails, thawed
- 1 tablespoon butter, melted
- ½ teaspoon Old Bay Seasoning
- 1 tablespoon chopped fresh parsley
- 2 lemon wedges

DIRECTIONS:

1. Preheat air fryer at 400°F for 3 minutes.
2. Using kitchen shears, cut down the middle of each lobster tail on the softer side. Carefully run your finger between the lobster meat and the shell to loosen meat.
3. Place lobster tails in ungreased air fryer basket, cut sides up. Cook 4 minutes. Brush with butter and sprinkle with Old Bay Seasoning. Cook an additional 4 minutes.
4. Serve warm, garnished with parsley and lemon wedges.

NUTRITION: Calories: 154 Protein: 21g Fiber: 0g Net carbohydrates: 1g Fat: 7g Sodium: 889mg Carbohydrates: 1g Sugar: 0g

53. Simply Shrimp

Preparation Time: 5 minutes

Cooking Time: 6 minutes

Servings: 2

INGREDIENTS:

- 1-pound medium raw shrimp, tail on, deveined, and thawed or fresh
- 2 tablespoons butter, melted
- 1 tablespoon fresh lemon juice (about ½ medium lemon)

DIRECTIONS:

1. Preheat air fryer at 350°F for 3 minutes.
2. In a large bowl, toss shrimp in butter.
3. Place shrimp in air fryer basket lightly greased with olive oil. Cook 4 minutes. Gently flip shrimp. Cook an additional 2 minutes.
4. Transfer shrimp to a large serving plate. Squeeze lemon juice over shrimp and serve.

NUTRITION: Calories: 265 Protein: 31g Fiber: 0g Net carbohydrates: 3g Fat: 14g Sodium: 1,285mg Carbohydrates: 3g Sugar: 0g

54. Crab Cakes With Arugula And Blackberry Salad

Preparation Time: 15 minutes

Cooking Time: 10 minutes

Servings: 2

INGREDIENTS:

- For Crab Cakes
- 8 ounces lump crabmeat, shells discarded
- 2 tablespoons mayonnaise
- ½ teaspoon Dijon mustard

- ½ teaspoon lemon juice
- 2 teaspoons peeled and minced yellow onion
- 1 4 teaspoon prepared horseradish
- 1 4 cup almond meal
- 1 large egg white, beaten
- ½ teaspoon Old Bay Seasoning
- For Salad
- 1 tablespoon olive oil
- 2 teaspoons lemon juice
- 1 eight teaspoon salt
- 1 eight teaspoons freshly ground black pepper
- 4 ounces fresh arugula
- ½ cup fresh blackberries
- 1 4 cup walnut pieces
- 2 lemon wedges

DIRECTIONS:

1. To make Crab Cakes: Preheat air fryer at 400°F for 3 minutes.
2. In a medium bowl, combine all ingredients. Form into four patties.
3. Place patties into air fryer basket lightly greased with olive oil. Cook 5 minutes. Flip patties. Cook an additional 5 minutes.
4. Transfer crab cakes to a large plate. Set aside.
5. To make Salad: In a large bowl, whisk together olive oil, lemon juice, salt, and pepper. Add arugula and toss. Distribute into two medium bowls.
6. Add two crab cakes to each bowl. Garnish with blackberries, walnuts, and lemon wedges. Serve.

NUTRITION: Calories: 406 Protein: 29g Fiber: 4g Net carbohydrates: 6g Fat: 29g Sodium: 790mg Carbohydrates: 10g Sugar: 4g

55. Steamer Clams

Preparation Time: 20 minutes

Cooking Time: 7 minutes

Servings: 2

INGREDIENTS:

- 25 littleneck clams, scrubbed
- 2 tablespoons water
- 2 tablespoons butter, melted
- 2 lemon wedges

DIRECTIONS:

1. Place clams in a large bowl filled with water. Let stand 10 minutes. Drain. Refill bowl with water and let stand an additional 10 minutes. Drain.

2. Preheat air fryer at 350°F for 3 minutes.

3. Pour 2 tablespoons water into bottom of air fryer. Add clams to ungreased air fryer basket. Cook 7 minutes. Discard any clams that don't open.

4. Remove clams from shells and add to a large serving dish with melted butter. Squeeze lemon on top and serve.

NUTRITION: Calories: 279 Protein: 30g Fiber: 0g Net carbohydrates: 7g Fat: 14g Sodium: 1,429mg

Carbohydrates: 7g Sugar: 0g

56. Oysters Rockefeller

Preparation Time: 10 minutes

Cooking Time: 16 minutes

Servings: 2

INGREDIENTS:

- 2 tablespoons butter
- 1 medium shallot, peeled and minced
- 1 clove garlic, peeled and minced
- 1 cup chopped fresh baby spinach
- 4 teaspoons grated Parmesan cheese
- 1 8 teaspoon Tabasco original hot sauce
- ½ teaspoon fresh lemon juice
- 1 4 cup crushed garlic pork rinds
- 12 oysters, on the half shell, rinsed and patted dry

DIRECTIONS:

1. In a small skillet, heat butter over medium heat 30 seconds. Add shallot, garlic, and spinach. Stir-fry 3 minutes until shallot is translucent.

2. Add Parmesan cheese, Tabasco sauce, lemon juice, and pork rinds to skillet. Distribute mixture to tops of oysters.

3. Preheat air fryer at 400°F for 3 minutes.

4. Place halves of oysters in ungreased air fryer basket. Cook 6 minutes.

5. Transfer cooked oysters to a large serving plate and repeat cooking with remaining oysters. Serve warm.

NUTRITION: Calories: 198 Protein: 9g Fiber: 1g Net carbohydrates: 5g Fat: 15g Sodium: 213mg

Carbohydrates: 6g Sugar: 2g

57. Crab-Stuffed Mushrooms

Preparation Time: 10 minutes

Cooking Time: 20 minutes

Servings: 6

INGREDIENTS:

- 2 ounces cream cheese, at room temperature
- ½ cup lump crabmeat, shells discarded
- 1 teaspoon prepared horseradish
- 1 teaspoon lemon juice
- ½ teaspoon salt
- ½ teaspoon freshly ground black pepper
- 16 ounces baby bell (cremini) mushrooms, stems removed
- 2 tablespoons panko bread crumbs
- 2 tablespoons butter, melted
- 1 4 cup chopped fresh parsley

DIRECTIONS:

1. In a medium bowl, combine cream cheese, crabmeat, horseradish, lemon juice, salt, and pepper.
2. Preheat air fryer at 350°F for 5 minutes.
3. Evenly stuff cream cheese mixture into mushroom caps. Distribute bread crumbs over stuffed mushrooms. Drizzle melted butter over bread crumbs.
4. Place halves of mushrooms in fryer basket. Cook 10 minutes. Transfer to serving plate. Repeat with remaining mushrooms.
5. Garnish with chopped parsley. Serve warm.

NUTRITION: Calories: 99 Protein: 5g Fiber: 1g Net carbohydrates: 4g Fat: 7g Sodium: 274mg
Carbohydrates: 5g Sugar: 2g

58. Salmon and Chive Pate

Preparation Time: 15 minutes
Cooking Time: 20 minutes
Servings: 3

INGREDIENTS:

- 100g soft white cheese spread e.g., Philadelphia
- 200g tin salmon, drained boned
- 1 4pt (150ml) mayonnaise
- 50g melted margarine
- Two tablespoons lemon juice
- Two tablespoons chopped chives

DIRECTIONS:

1. 1.Blend the soft cream cheese, mayonnaise, salmon, and lemon juice until mixed. Add the melted margarine gradually and mix properly.
2. 2.Stir in the chives. Pour it into ramekins and refrigerate.
3. In brief

4. Salt, potassium, and fluid are the most vital considerations. If you are on a fluid restriction, take special care. All drinks (cold, hot, and alcoholic), fruit juices, jellies, soups, ice lollies, and ice cream must be included in your daily allowance.
5. An average jelly = 150ml
6. An average portion of soup = 250ml
7. An average ice cube = 25ml
8. An average ice cream scoop = 75ml
9. Avoid salty snacks e.g., crisps, nuts, etc. These will make you thirstier.

NUTRITION: Calories 147 Fat: 6.5g Fiber: 2.4g Carbs: 12.8g Protein: 2.9g

59. Creole Red Fish Bites

Preparation Time: 20 minutes

Cooking Time: 25-30 minutes

Servings: 8-10

INGREDIENTS:

- 1 (5- to 6-pound) red fish Cheesecloth
- 1-quart mayonnaise (reserve enough for icing)
- 1 bottle horseradish
- 1 clove garlic, pressed
- 1 2 medium onion, grated
- 1 teaspoon dry mustard
- 1 large carrot, chopped fine or grated
- 1 large dill pickle, chopped
- 1 bottle capers, drained
- Worcestershire sauce
- Tabasco, red pepper, salt, and black pepper to taste
- Juice of 1 2 lemon

DIRECTIONS:

1. Have the head removed from the fish. Place fish on the cheesecloth, tying at each end. Have the cloth long enough to extend out of the very large pot you will need to poach the fish. This is for easy removal. Poach the fish in well-seasoned water, preferably seasoned with crab boil, salt, lemon, black pepper, and red pepper. When fish is done, remove, cool, and flake. Mix the fish meat with the above-listed ingredients, reserving enough mayonnaise to ice the fish after shaping. Check seasonings according to taste. The fish may be put in fish mold(s), or one large fish may be shaped on a platter. Ice with mayonnaise and decorate with lemon slices for fins, and a stuffed olive for the eye. Serve with crackers.

NUTRITION: Calories 147 Fat: 6.5g Fiber: 2.4g Carbs: 12.8g Protein: 2.9g

60. Blackened Potato Crusted Shrimp

Preparation Time: 15 minutes

Cooking Time: 10 minutes

Servings: 4

INGREDIENTS:

- 1 lb. jumbo shrimp, shelled and deveined
- 1 tsp blackening seasoning
- 2 C. frozen Hash Browns
- 2 tbsp vegetable oil
- 1 small lemon

DIRECTIONS:

2. Toss in it the shrimp with Cajun blackening seasoning in a bowl.
3. Place a large pan over medium heat. Heat the oil in it. Press the potato hash into the shrimp then cook them in the hot oil for 4 to 5 min on each side.
4. Squeeze over them some fresh lemon juice.
5. Enjoy.

NUTRITION: Calories 165 Fat: 7.5g Fiber: 2.9g Carbs: 12.5g Protein: 7.1.g

61. Crispy Oysters

Preparation Time: 20 minutes

Cooking Time: 15 minutes

Servings: 4

INGREDIENTS:

- 3 4 cup all-purpose flour
- 1 8 tsp. salt
- 1 8 tsp. pepper
- 2 large eggs
- 1 cup dry bread crumbs
- 2 3 cup grated Romano cheese
- 1 4 cup minced fresh parsley
- 1 2 tsp. garlic salt
- 1-pint shucked oysters
- 2 tbsps. olive oil
- JALAPENO MAYONNAISE:
- 1 4 cup mayonnaise
- 1 4 cup sour cream
- 2 medium jalapeno peppers, seeded and finely chopped
- 2 tbsps. milk

- 1 tsp. lemon juice
- 1 4 tsp. grated lemon peel
- 1 8 tsp. salt
- 1 8 tsp. pepper

DIRECTIONS:

1. Mix together pepper, salt, and flour in a shallow bowl. Whisk eggs in a separate shallow bowl. Mix together garlic salt, parsley, cheese, and bread crumbs in a third bowl. Use flour mixture to coat oysters, then coat them with eggs and then with crumb mixture. Arrange in a 15"x10"x1" baking pan coated with grease, then drizzle oil over the top. Bake at 400 degrees until turn golden brown, about 15 minutes. In the meantime, whisk jalapeno mayonnaise ingredients together in a small bowl, then serve together with oysters.

NUTRITION: Calories 297 Fat: 16.7g Fiber: 6.9g Carbs: 34.5g Protein: 15.g

62. Cajun Bbq Shrimps

Preparation Time: 10 minutes

Cooking Time: 15 minutes

Servings: 4

INGREDIENTS:

- 1 lb. unsalted butter
- 2 T paprika
- 3 T Lea & Perrins Worcestershire Sauce
- 1 T garlic powder
- 1 t salt
- 8 T lemon juice
- 2 T barbeque seasoning
- 2 lbs. large shrimp
- Optional: Cayenne pepper to taste

DIRECTIONS:

1. All the ingredients will be mixed together and simmered. Then add the shrimp, heads off, peels on, and cook for 10 to 15 minutes until done. Serve with French bread to dip into the sauce, and a salad

NUTRITION: Calories 140 Fat: 2.5g Fiber: 3.8g Carbs: 13.4g Protein: 12.7g

63. Southern Stuffed Artichokes

Preparation Time: 40 minutes

Cooking Time: 3-4 hrs.

Servings: 10

INGREDIENTS:

- 10 whole artichokes

- 1 cup Italian seasoned bread crumbs
- 4 oz. provolone cheese, shredded
- 10 pimento-stuffed green olives, chopped
- 1 2 bunch fresh parsley, chopped
- 5 cloves garlic, minced
- 1 bunch green onions, finely chopped
- 2 small stalks celery, finely chopped
- 1 2 green bell pepper, finely chopped
- 1 tsp. lemon juice
- 1 tsp. hot pepper sauce
- 4 (2 oz.) cans anchovy fillets, chopped
- 1 tsp. Worcestershire sauce
- 1 tbsp. olive oil, or as needed
- salt to taste

DIRECTIONS:

2. To prepare artichokes, cut off the bottoms of stems and trim the tips of leaves. To trim leaves, scissors is the best choice. Tear off small leaves around base and throw them away.

3. In a big pot, add artichokes and enough amount of water to cover. On top of them, put a dinner plate to prevent the artichokes from floating out of water. Place a lid on pot to cover and bring to a boil. Boil until there are some leaves floating in the water, about 10-15 minutes, then drain and cool artichokes.

4. Combine bell pepper, celery, green onions, garlic, parsley, olives, cheese and bread crumbs together in a medium bowl. Stir salt, olive oil, Worcestershire sauce, anchovies, hot pepper sauce and lemon juice together in a small bowl, then stir into the bread crumb mixture.

5. Tear off a big square of aluminum foil for each artichoke. Put one artichoke in the center of each square and tuck approximately 1 2 tsp. of the cheese mixture under each leaf. Gather up foil around artichoke and leave top opening.

6. In bottom of a big pot, set a wire rack or steamer insert, then fill with 3 in. of fresh water or so that artichokes remain above water level. Place artichokes upright in the pot and bring to a boil. Place on a cover and allow artichokes to steam about 3 hours. Take out of the pot and let them cool to room temperature prior to serving.

NUTRITION: Calories 218 Fat: 6g Fiber: 8.4g Carbs: 28g Protein:7.3g

64. __Number 0louisiana Shrimp Boil__

Preparation Time: 30-40 minutes

Cooking Time: 30-45 minutes

Servings: 10

INGREDIENTS:

- 1 (3 oz.) bags shrimp
- 3 tbsp Old Bay Seasoning
- 3 lbs. new potatoes

- 5 ears corn, husked and cut into 3 pieces each
- 2 lbs. smoked link sausage
- 4 lbs. large unpeeled shrimp
- 4 lemons
- 2 tbsp liquid egg product
- 1 tbsp cider vinegar
- 1 tbsp lemon juice
- 1 tsp kosher salt
- 1 tsp ground mustard
- 1 1 2 C. peanut oil
- 1 tsp garlic
- 1 tbsp boiling water

DIRECTIONS:

1. In a container or bowl, whisk the egg product, lemon juice, salt, and mustard.
2. Add the oil gradually while mixing them all the time for 8 min until the mix becomes thick. Stir in the garlic with a pinch of salt into the sauce. Whisk into it 1 tbsp of boiling water and let it sit for 3 min then place it in the fridge. Heat in it 2 gallons of water until it starts boiling.
3. Stir in it the shrimp with old bay seasoning. Cook them for 12 min over low heat. Stir in the potatoes and cook it for 9 min.
4. Stir in the corn and cook them for an extra 6 min
5. Add the unpeeled shrimp and sausage to the pot. Cook them for 5 min. Drain all the cooked ingredients and place them on a serving plate with the peanut sauce.
6. Enjoy.

NUTRITION: Calories 233 Fat: 11.9g Fiber: 12g Carbs: 38.1g Protein: 15.1g

65. Number 0 Cornmeal Crusted Catfish With Lemon-Thyme Mayo

Preparation Time: 15 minutes

Cooking Time: 15 minutes

Servings: 4-6

INGREDIENTS:

- Nonstick cooking spray
- ½ cup dry bread crumbs
- ½ cup cornmeal
- 1 teaspoon Old Bay seasoning
- 1 4 teaspoon salt
- 1 4 teaspoon cayenne pepper
- 1 4 cup finely chopped pecans, toasted
- 1 tablespoon cooking oil

- 4 (4-ounce) catfish fillets
- 1 large egg, beaten
- FOR THE SAUCE
- 1 4 cup mayonnaise
- 3 tablespoons freshly squeezed lemon juice
- 2 tablespoons minced fresh lemon thyme

DIRECTIONS:

1. Preheat the oven to 500°F. In a shallow bowl, stir together the bread crumbs, cornmeal, Old Bay seasoning, salt, and cayenne until blended. Mix in the pecans. Add the oil to the pecan–bread crumb mixture. Stir to combine. Brush each catfish fillet lightly with beaten egg. Dredge fillet into the bread crumb mixture to coat on both sides. Pu fillets in the baking dish. Bake, uncovered, for 6 to 8 minutes for each ½ inch of thickness, or until the fish flakes easily with a fork.
2. TO MAKE THE SAUCE
3. While the fish is baking, mix the mayonnaise, lemon juice, and fresh lemon thyme until blended. Serve with the catfish.

NUTRITION: Calories 198.4 Fat: 12.1g Fiber: 8.4gg Carbs: 28.4g Protein: 12.8g

66. Crawfish Etouffee

Preparation Time: 30 minutes

Cooking Time: 1 hr. and 10 minutes

Servings: 6

INGREDIENTS:

- 1 fourth-pound butter
- 2 onions, chopped
- 2 ribs celery, chopped
- 3 toes garlic, minced
- 1 bell pepper, chopped
- 1 2 cup chopped green onions
- 1 tablespoon tomato paste
- 1 4 teaspoon thyme
- 1 2 cup water
- 2 ½ tablespoons flour
- 1 2 teaspoon basil
- 1 4 teaspoon ground cloves
- 1 4 teaspoon chili powder
- 1 tablespoon lemon juice
- 1 3 cup crawfish water
- Salt and pepper to taste
- 2 tablespoons minced parsley

DIRECTIONS:

1. Melt butter in a pan then put the flour and cook until the color becomes light brown. Put in the celery, onions, garlic, bell pepper then continue sautéing it until veggies are

2. soft. Add the tomato paste, crawfish tails, thyme, basil, cloves, chili powder, lemon juice, crawfish water, and water. Mix well and cook about 15 minutes. Add salt and pepper to taste. Cover and let simmer another 10 minutes. Add the green onions and parsley.

3. Remove from the heat and let stand a minimum of 10 minutes with cover.

NUTRITION: Calories 218 Fat: 3.4g Fiber: 10g Carbs: 25.5g Protein: 9g

67. Greek Penne And Chicken

Preparation Time: 15 minutes

Cooking Time: 15 minutes

Servings: 4

INGREDIENTS

- 16-ounce package of Penne Pasta
- 1 pound of Skinless Boneless Chicken Breast Halves (Cut into Bite Sized Pieces)
- 1 half cup of Chopped Red Onion
- 1 1 2 tablespoons of Butter
- 2 cloves of Minced Garlic
- 14-ounce can of Artichoke Hearts
- 1 Chopped Tomato
- 3 tablespoons of Chopped Fresh Parsley
- 1 half cup of Crumbled Feta Cheese
- 2 tablespoons of Lemon Juice
- 1 teaspoon of Dried Oregano
- Ground Black Pepper
- Salt

DIRECTIONS:

1. In a large sized skillet over a medium-high heat, melt your butter. Add your garlic and onion. Cook approximately 2 minutes. Add your chopped chicken and continue to cook until golden brown. Should take approximately 5 to 6 minutes. Stir occasionally.
2. Reduce your heat to a medium-low. Drain and chop your artichoke hearts. Add them to your skillet along with your chopped tomato, fresh parsley, feta cheese, dried oregano, lemon juice, and drained pasta. Cook for 2 to 3 minutes until heated through.
3. Season with your ground black pepper and salt.
4. Serve and Enjoy!

NUTRITION: Calories 218 Fat: 3.4g Fiber: 10g Carbs: 25.5g Protein: 9g

68. Yogurt-Marinated Chicken Kebabs

Preparation Time: 15 minutes

Cooking Time: 15 minutes

Servings: 4

INGREDIENTS:

- ½ cup plain Greek yogurt
- 1 tablespoon lemon juice
- ½ teaspoon ground cumin
- ½ teaspoon ground coriander
- ½ teaspoon kosher salt
- 1 4 teaspoon cayenne pepper
- 1½ pound skinless, boneless chicken breast, cut into 1-inch cubes

DIRECTIONS:

1. In a large bowl or zip-top bag, combine the yogurt, lemon juice, cumin, coriander, salt, and cayenne pepper. Mix together thoroughly and then add the chicken. Marinate for at least 30 minutes, and up to overnight in the refrigerator.
2. Bake for 20 minutes, turning the chicken over once halfway through the cooking time.

NUTRITION: Calories 218 Fat: 3.4g Fiber: 10g Carbs: 25.5g Protein: 9g

69. Crispy Mediterranean Chicken Thighs

Preparation Time: 15 minutes

Cooking Time: 35 minutes

Servings: 6

INGREDIENTS:

- 2 tablespoons extra-virgin olive oil
- 2 teaspoons dried rosemary
- 1½ teaspoons ground cumin
- 1½ teaspoons ground coriander
- ¾ teaspoon dried oregano

- 1 8 teaspoon salt
- 6 bone-in, skin-on chicken thighs (about 3 pounds)

DIRECTIONS

1. Preheat the oven to 450°F. Line a baking sheet with parchment paper.
2. Place the olive oil and spices into a large bowl and mix together, making a paste. Add the chicken and mix together until evenly coated. Place on the prepared baking sheet.
3. Bake for 30 to 35 minutes, or until golden brown and the chicken registers an internal temperature of 165°F.

NUTRITION: Calories 218 Fat: 3.4g Fiber: 10g Carbs: 25.5g Protein: 9g

70. **High-Quality Belizean Chicken Stew**

Preparation Time: 15 minutes

Cooking Time: 25 minutes

Servings: 4

INGREDIENTS

- 4 whole chicken
- 1 tablespoon coconut oil
- 2 tablespoons achiote seasoning
- 2 tablespoons white vinegar
- 3 tablespoons Worcestershire sauce
- 1 cup yellow onion, sliced
- 3 garlic cloves, sliced
- 1 teaspoon ground cumin
- 1 teaspoon dried oregano
- ½ teaspoon black pepper
- 2 cups chicken stock

DIRECTIONS

1. Take a large sized bowl and add achiote paste, vinegar, Worcestershire sauce, oregano, cumin and pepper. Mix well and add chicken pieces and rub the marinade all over them
2. Allow the chicken to sit overnight. Set your skillet to Sauté mode and add coconut oil
3. Once the oil is hot, add the chicken pieces to the skillet and brown them in batches (each batch for 2 minutes). Remove the seared chicken and transfer them to a plate
4. Add onions, garlic to the skillet and Sauté for 2-3 minutes. Add chicken pieces back to the skillet
5. Pour chicken broth to the bowl with marinade and stir well. Add the mixture to the skillet
6. Seal up the lid and cook for about 20 minutes at high pressure
7. Once done, release the pressure naturally. Season with a bit of salt and serve!

NUTRITION: Calories 218 Fat: 3.4g Fiber: 10g Carbs: 25.5g Protein: 9g

71. Garlic And Lemon Chicken Dish

Preparation Time: 15 minutes

Cooking Time: 25 minutes

Servings: 4

INGREDIENTS

- 2-3 pounds chicken breast
- 1 teaspoon salt
- 1 onion, diced
- 1 tablespoon ghee
- 5 garlic cloves, minced
- ½ cup organic chicken broth
- 1 teaspoon dried parsley
- 1 large lemon, juiced
- 3-4 teaspoon arrowroot flour

DIRECTIONS

1. Set your skillet to Sauté mode. Add diced up onion and cooking fat
2. Allow the onions to cook for 5 -10 minutes
3. Add the rest of the ingredients except arrowroot flour
4. Lock up the lid and set the skillet to poultry mode. Cook until the timer runs out
5. Allow the pressure to release naturally
6. Once done, remove 1 fourth cup of the sauce from the skillet and add arrowroot to make a slurry
7. Add the slurry to the skillet to make the gravy thick. Keep stirring well. Serve!

NUTRITION: Calories 218 Fat: 3.4g Fiber: 10g Carbs: 25.5g Protein: 9g

72. Honey Balsamic Chicken

Preparation Time: 25 minutes

Cooking Time: 35 minutes

Servings: 10

INGREDIENTS:

- 1 4 cup honey
- 1 2 cup balsamic vinegar
- 1 4 cup soy sauce
- 2 cloves garlic minced
- 10 chicken drumsticks

DIRECTIONS

1. Mix the honey, vinegar, soy sauce and garlic in a bowl.
2. Marinate the chicken in the sauce for 30 minutes.
3. Cover the skillet.

4. Set it to manual.
5. Cook at high pressure for 10 minutes.
6. Release the pressure quickly.
7. Choose the sauté button to thicken the sauce.

NUTRITION: Calories 218 Fat: 3.4g Fiber: 10g Carbs: 45.5g Protein: 9g

73. <u>Chicken Shawarma</u>

Preparation Time: 25 minutes

Cooking Time: 15 minutes

Servings: 8

INGREDIENTS:

- 2 lb. chicken breast, sliced into strips
- 1 teaspoon paprika
- 1 teaspoon ground cumin
- 1 4 teaspoon granulated garlic
- 1 2 teaspoon turmeric
- 1 4 teaspoon ground allspice

DIRECTIONS

1. Season the chicken with the spices, and a little salt and pepper.
2. Pour 1 cup chicken broth to the skillet.
3. Seal the skillet.
4. Choose poultry setting.
5. Cook for 15 minutes.
6. Release the pressure naturally.

NUTRITION: Calories 218 Fat: 3.4g Fiber: 10g Carbs: 45.5g Protein: 9g

74. Buffalo-Style Pork Meatballs

Preparation Time: 15 minutes

Cooking Time: 16 minutes

Servings: 4

INGREDIENTS:

- 1-pound ground pork
- 1 large egg
- 1 fourth cup buffalo wing sauce
- 1 fourth cup grated celery
- 1 fourth cup finely chopped fresh parsley
- 1 fourth cup almond flour
- 1 fourth teaspoon saltDirections:

DIRECTIONS

1. Preheat air fryer at 350°F for 3 minutes.
2. Combine all ingredients in a large bowl. Form into sixteen meatballs.
3. Add eight meatballs to air fryer basket lightly greased with olive oil and cook 6 minutes. Flip and cook an additional 2 minutes.
4. Transfer cooked meatballs to a large serving plate. Repeat cooking with remaining meatballs. Serve warm.

NUTRITION: Calories: 303 Protein: 24g Fiber: 1g Net carbohydrates: 1g Fat: 22g Sodium: 583mg

Carbohydrates: 2g Sugar: 1g

75. Peach Barbecue Pork Chops

Preparation Time: 5 minutes

Cooking Time: 12 minutes

Servings: 2

INGREDIENTS:

- 2 tablespoons sugar-free peach
- 2 tablespoons no-sugar-added tomato paste
- 1 tablespoon Dijon mustard
- 1 teaspoon Worcestershire sauce
- 1 tablespoon fresh lemon juice
- 1 tablespoon olive oil
- 2 cloves garlic, peeled and minced
- 2 (1"-thick) bone-in pork chops

DIRECTIONS:

1. In a medium bowl, whisk together peach, tomato paste, Dijon mustard, Worcestershire sauce, lemon juice, olive oil, and garlic. Add pork chops to mixture and toss. Refrigerate covered 30 minutes.
2. Preheat air fryer at 350°F for 3 minutes.
3. Place pork chops in ungreased air fryer basket. Cook 4 minutes. Flip and cook 4 more minutes. Flip once more and cook an additional 4 minutes. Using a meat thermometer, ensure internal temperature is at least 145°F.
4. Transfer pork to a cutting board and let rest 5 minutes before serving warm.

NUTRITION: Calories: 374 Protein: 28g Fiber: 1g Net carbohydrates: 5g Fat: 22g Sodium: 277mg
Carbohydrates: 18g Sugar: 3g

76. Flank Steak With Creamy Horseradish Sauce

Preparation Time: 10 minutes

Cooking Time: 9 minutes

Servings: 2

INGREDIENTS:

- For Creamy Horseradish Sauce
- 2 tablespoons prepared horseradish
- 2 tablespoons plain Greek yogurt
- 2 tablespoons mayonnaise
- 1 tablespoon fresh lemon juice
- 1 eight teaspoon salt
- 1 eight teaspoons freshly ground black pepper
- ½ teaspoon Worcestershire sauce

1. **DIRECTIONS:**

    For Flank Steak

2. 1 (12-ounce) flank steak, cut in half

3. 2 tablespoons olive oil

4. 1 teaspoon salt

5. ½ teaspoon freshly ground black pepper

6. To make Creamy Horseradish Sauce: Whisk together all ingredients in a small bowl and refrigerate covered until ready to use.

7. To make Flank Steak: Preheat air fryer at 400°F for 3 minutes.

8. Rub flank steak halves with olive oil. Season with salt and pepper.

9. Place steaks in ungreased air fryer basket. Cook 4 minutes. Flip and cook an additional 5 minutes or until desired doneness.

10. Transfer steaks to a cutting board and let rest 5 minutes, then thinly slice against the grain and place on two medium plates.

11. Drizzle horseradish sauce over steaks and serve immediately.

NUTRITION: Calories: 480 Protein: 36g Fiber: 1g Net carbohydrates: 4g Fat: 35g Sodium: 1,547mg

Carbohydrates: 5g Sugar: 2g

77. T-Bone With Garlic Rosemary Compound Butter

Preparation Time: 10 minutes

Cooking Time: 10 minutes

Servings: 2

INGREDIENTS:

- 2 tablespoons butter, softened
- 1 4 teaspoon lemon juice
- 2 cloves garlic, peeled and minced
- 1 teaspoon minced fresh rosemary
- 1 (20-ounce, 11 4"-thick)
- T-bone steak, fat trimmed, leaving a 1 4" ribbon
- 1 teaspoon salt
- ½ teaspoon freshly ground black pepper
- 2 tablespoons water

DIRECTIONS:

1. Combine butter, lemon juice, garlic, and rosemary in a small bowl. Transfer butter onto parchment paper or plastic wrap. Roll into a log, spinning ends to tighten. Refrigerate 2 hours up to overnight.

2. Remove T-bone from refrigerator 30 minutes before cooking. Season with salt and pepper.

3. Preheat air fryer at 400°F for 3 minutes. Add 2 tablespoons water to air fryer.

4. Place steak in air fryer basket lightly greased with olive oil. Cook 5 minutes. Flip steak and cook an additional 5 minutes until a meat thermometer ensures an internal temperature of at least 135°F, or meat reaches desired doneness.

5. Transfer steak to a cutting board and let rest 5 minutes. Slice butter and add to top of steak. Let melt over meat. Serve warm.

NUTRITION: Calories: 627 Protein: 45g Fiber: 0g Net carbohydrates: 1g Fat: 48g Sodium: 1,276mg Carbohydrates: 2g Sugar: 0g

78. Grilled Chicken Cobb Salad

Preparation Time: 10 minutes

Cooking Time: 18 minutes

Servings: 4

INGREDIENTS:

- 2 (approximately ½-pound) boneless, skinless chicken breasts, cut into 1" cubes
- 1 tablespoon avocado oil
- ½ teaspoon salt
- 1 fourth teaspoon freshly ground black pepper
- 4 cups chopped romaine lettuce
- 2 tablespoons olive oil
- 1 tablespoon fresh lemon juice
- 2 Air-Fried Hard "Boiled" Eggs, sliced
- 4 pieces sugar-free bacon, cooked and crumbled
- 2 medium Roma tomatoes, cored, seeded, and diced
- 1 4 cup blue cheese crumbles
- 1 fourth cup peeled and diced red onion
- 1 large avocado, peeled, pitted, and diced

DIRECTIONS:

1. Preheat air fryer at 350°F for 3 minutes.
2. In a large bowl, toss chicken cubes with avocado oil. Season with salt and pepper.
3. Add half of chicken cubes to ungreased air fryer basket. Cook 4 minutes. Shake gently and flip chicken. Cook an additional 5 minutes. Using a meat thermometer, ensure internal temperature is at least 165°F.
4. Transfer cooked chicken to a large plate. Repeat cooking with remaining chicken.
5. In a separate large bowl, toss romaine lettuce with olive oil and lemon juice. Distribute into four medium bowls.
6. Garnish salads with remaining ingredients, including cooked chicken. Serve.

NUTRITION: Calories: 427 Protein: 35g Fiber: 5g Net carbohydrates: 5g Fat: 28g Sodium: 632mg Carbohydrates: 9g Sugar: 3g

79. Fried Artichoke Hearts

Preparation Time: 10 minutes

Cooking Time: 14 minutes

Servings: 4

INGREDIENTS:

- 1 large egg
- 1 tablespoon Dijon mustard
- ½ cup crushed pork rinds
- 1 4 cup almond flour
- 1 (14.75-ounce) jar artichoke hearts in water, drained

DIRECTIONS:

1. Preheat air fryer at 350°F for 3 minutes.
2. In a medium bowl, whisk together egg and Dijon mustard.
3. In a separate shallow dish combine pork rinds and almond flour.
4. Dip artichoke hearts in egg mixture, then dredge in pork rind mixture.
5. Place half of prepared artichoke hearts in ungreased air fryer basket. Cook 7 minutes.
6. Transfer to a large serving plate and repeat cooking with remaining artichokes. Serve warm.

NUTRITION: Calories: 107 Protein: 7g Fiber: 1g Net carbohydrates: 2g Fat: 6g Sodium: 342mg
Carbohydrates: 6g Sugar: 0g

80. Kedgeree

Preparation Time: 10 minutes

Cooking Time: 14 minutes

Servings: 4

- **INGREDIENTS:**
  ½ onion finely sliced
- 200g (7oz) long grain rice
- One tbsp of vegetable or olive oil
- 400g (14oz) poached smoked haddock or cod filets
- Two teaspoons curry powder
- Four hard boiled eggs
- ½ a lemon
- 400ml low salt chicken stock

DIRECTIONS:

1. Warm the oil in a big frying pan, add the onion and fry until softened. To coat the rice in the oil, add the curry powder and rice and stir. Add the water or stock. Cover with a tight-fitting lid or tin foil and allow to boil on a low heat until most of the water has been absorbed (about 10 minutes).

2. Place the fish and quartered eggs on top of the rice and replace the lid when most of the water has been absorbed. Continue to cook for another few minutes on the lowest heat and then turn off the heat, leaving the covered rice, fish and eggs to steam for five - ten minutes, allowing the fish to warm through the lid. Remove the lid when after 5 - 10 minutes, and fork the fish with a squeeze of lemon juice into the rice.

NUTRITION: Calories: 107 Protein: 7g Fiber: 1g Net Carbohydrates: 2g Fat: 6g Sodium: 342mg
Carbohydrates: 6g Sugar: 0g

81. Chicken And Lemon Casserole

Preparation Time: 20 minutes

Cooking Time: 19 minutes

Servings: 4

INGREDIENTS:

- 2 tablespoons of honey
- One lemon, zest and juice only, plus one lemon, sliced into thin rounds
- freshly ground black pepper and salt
- 80g (3oz) butter
- 2kg (4lb 4oz) skinless chicken thighs or drumsticks
- Two tsp of dried thyme (optional)
- 500ml hot low salt chicken stock
- One tbsp of vegetable or olive oil
- Four garlic cloves crushed

DIRECTIONS:

1. Preheat the oven to 200°C (180°C Fan) Gas 6 400°F.
2. Place the lemon zest, lemon juice, and honey into a bowl and whisk until well mixed. Add the chicken pieces and stir until they are fully coated in the mixture. Set aside for ten minutes to marinate.
3. Heat 40g 1½oz of the butter and half of the olive oil in a flame proof casserole pan over a medium heat. Add half of the marinated chicken pieces when the butter is foaming, and fry for five - six minutes, turning periodically, until golden-brown. Put the chicken pieces aside and repeat this process with the remaining chicken pieces and butter oil then set the chicken aside again.
4. Add the lemon slices, garlic cloves, and residual marinade juices to the pan and stir properly, scraping any burned bits off the base of the pan with a wooden spoon. Return the cooked chicken to the pan, add the hot chicken stock and thyme, then stir properly. Take the mixture to the boil, put inside the oven to cook for thirty minutes, or until the chicken is cooked through.
5. Remove the pieces of chicken from the pan and set them aside on a warm plate. Strain the sauce into a saucepan through a fine sieve, using the back of a wooden spoon to press the garlic pulp through the sieve. Simmer the lemon sauce for another five - ten minutes over high heat.
6. Spoon the lemon sauce over the casseroled chicken, then serve.

NUTRITION: Calories 107 Protein 7 Fiber 3 Fats 6 Carbohydrates 6

82. Skewers Of Seitan

Preparation Time: 15 minutes

Cooking Time: 20 minutes

Servings: 6

INGREDIENTS:

- 1 block of seitan 240 g
- 1 lemon
- 3 tablespoons sesame oil
- 2 onions
- 1 clove of garlic
- 1 tablespoon acacia honey
- 1 tablespoon paprika
- 200 g cherry tomatoes
- 100 g of Paris mushrooms
- 2 tablespoons sesame seeds
- Salt pepper

DIRECTION:

1. Wash the lemon under running water, sponge it, and squeeze it.
2. Peel the onions, slice them. Peel and slice the clove of garlic.
3. Cut the seitan into cubes.
4. Mix honey and lemon juice, add oil and paprika, salt, and pepper. Arrange the seitan, onions, and garlic in a dish and sprinkle with the marinade. Allow in the refrigerator for at least 1 hour.
5. Wash the tomatoes and mushrooms, sponge them out. Cut the mushrooms into strips.
6. Make skewers by alternating seitan cubes with onion rings, cherry tomatoes, and mushroom slices. Filter the marinade.
7. Cook the kebabs on a pan in their marinade, 2 min 30 on each side over medium heat. Drain them and roll them in the sesame seeds. Iron for 1 min in the pan, just time to lightly brown the sesame seeds.

NUTRITION: Calories 107 Protein 7 Fiber 3 Fats 6Carbohydrates 6

83. Chicken Soup

Preparation Time: 20 minutes

Cooking Time: 15 minutes

Servings: 4

INGREDIENTS:

- One tbsp of vegetable or olive oil
- Two medium potatoes, peeled
- One-liter low salt chicken stock
- One leek

- Three medium carrots
- One tbsp cornflower (if required, see below)
- Squeeze of lemon juice
- Three tbsp Greek yogurt or double cream
- 300g (10½oz) leftover roast chicken, shredded and skin removed

DIRECTIONS:

1. Roughly chop the carrots, potatoes, and leek and boil in a large pot of water.
2. Drain the potatoes and vegetables (don't reuse the cooking water), return to the pot and add the stock.
3. Blend the soup with a blender to your preferred consistency.
4. If you want to make your soup thicker: on a low heat, return the pan to the hob, blend the cornflower with a dash of cold water and add to the soup. Stir constantly until the soup thickens when simmering. Add the chicken and leave for five minutes to cook. Add the cream or yogurt and the lemon juice to finish.

NUTRITION: Calories 107 Protein 7 Fiber 3 Fats 6 Carbohydrates 6

DANG GOOD SAUCES

84. Sautéed Shrimp

Preparation Time: 15 minutes

Cooking Time: 10 minutes

Servings: 4

INGREDIENTS:

- 1-pound medium shrimp
- ½ teaspoon sea salt
- 1 fourth teaspoon freshly ground black pepper
- 2 tablespoons extra-virgin olive oil or unsalted butter
- Juice of 1 lemon
- 1 recipe sauce

DIRECTIONS:

1. ADOBO: Add the shrimp as instructed in the recipe, and finish by following that recipe.
1. Peel and devein the shrimp, and season with salt and pepper.
2. In a large skillet over medium-high heat, heat the olive oil or butter until it shimmers (oil) or bubbles (butter).

3. Add the shrimp and cook, stirring, until they are bright pink and opaque, about 4 minutes. Add the lemon juice and cook, stirring, for 4 minutes more.

NUTRITION: Calories 37 Protein 7 Fiber 3 Fats 6 Carbohydrates 6

85. Chunky Avocado Sauce

Preparation Time: 15 minutes

Cooking Time: 5 minutes

Servings: 5

INGREDIENTS:

- 1 4 cup tomatoes, peeled, seeded, and chopped
- ½ cup shallots, minced
- 1 4 cup bell pepper, seeded, deveined, and minced
- 1 tablespoon chopped fresh parsley
- 1 to 2 garlic cloves, crushed
- 1 4 cup white wine vinegar
- 1 teaspoon salt
- Dash freshly ground black pepper
- Dash hot sauce
- ¾ cup puréed avocado
- ¾ cup chopped avocado

DIRECTIONS:

In a large mixing bowl, combine the tomatoes, shallots, bell pepper, parsley, garlic, vinegar, salt, pepper, hot sauce, and avocado. Mash together with the back of a spoon until the consistency is even.

2. Keep in the fridge until ready to serve.

STORAGE: 1 week in the refrigerator in a glass jar (pour a thin layer of lemon juice on top to help preserve it)

REPURPOSING TIP: Combine this sauce on a salad with equal parts oil and balsamic vinegar for a salad dressing.

NUTRITION: Calories 17 Protein3 Fiber 1 Fats 4 Carbohydrates 11

86. Green Salsa

Preparation Time: 20 minutes

Cooking Time: 20 minutes

Servings: 2 cups

INGREDIENTS:

- 3 tablespoons extra-virgin olive oil, divided
- 1 pound (about 16) ripe tomatillos, husked
- 2 chipotle chiles in adobo
- ½ green bell pepper, diced

- ½ red bell pepper, diced
- 2 shallots, chopped
- 5 garlic cloves, sliced
- 1 teaspoon ground cumin
- 1 teaspoon ground coriander
- Salt
- 1 small bunch fresh parsley, chopped
- 2 scallions, green parts only, chopped
- 1 small handful pine nuts, crushed
- SPECIAL EQUIPMENT NEEDED
- Food processor

DIRECTIONS:

1. In a large brazier or heavy covered skillet over medium heat, heat 2 tablespoons of olive oil. Add the tomatillos and fry for about 10 to 15 minutes, rotating occasionally, until soft and a little charred on all sides.
2. In a medium pan over medium heat, heat the remaining tablespoon of olive oil. Add the chipotle chiles, green and red peppers, shallots, and garlic, and sauté until the shallots turn golden brown, about 5 minutes. Mix in the cumin and coriander and a healthy pinch of salt.
3. In the food processor, combine the pepper mixture with the softened tomatillos, and pulse or use the chop setting.
4. Transfer to a bowl. Garnish with the parsley, scallions, and pine nuts, and season with salt.
1. STORAGE: 1 week in the refrigerator in a glass jar or plastic container or 1 month in the freezer in a plastic freezer bag or container
2. REPURPOSING TIP: Use this hot on pasta or cooked meat, or let cool for a divine salsa. Throw in a couple of chopped tomatoes or 4 ounces of tomato paste with a little cream to make a more robust pasta sauce.

NUTRITION: Calories 17 Protein3 Fiber 1 Fats 4 Carbohydrates 11

87. Smoky Hot Bbq Sauce

Preparation Time: 10 minutes

Cooking Time: 25 minutes

Servings: 2 CUPS

INGREDIENTS:

- 6 teaspoons coconut oil, divided
- 1 shallot, chopped
- 2 scallions, green parts only, chopped
- 2 garlic cloves, minced
- 3 Scotch bonnet or habanero chiles, stemmed and seeded (see Ingredient tip)
- 1 4 cup tomato paste

- ½ cup chicken or vegetable stock, or water
- 2 teaspoons ground allspice
- ½ cup fresh pineapple chunks
- 2 tablespoons soy sauce
- 1 4 cup apple cider vinegar
- 1 4 cup brown sugar
- 1 teaspoon salt
- 2 tablespoons honey
- Juice and zest of 1 lime
- SPECIAL EQUIPMENT NEEDED
- Food processor

DIRECTIONS:

1. In a medium skillet over medium heat, heat 2 teaspoons of oil. When hot, add the shallot, scallions, garlic, and chiles, and sauté until golden, 4 to 5 minutes.
2. Add the tomato paste and stock. Mix and cook until everything comes together, about 5 minutes.
3. Mix in the allspice, pineapple, soy sauce, vinegar, sugar, and salt. Stir. Then turn off the heat and let cool for 10 minutes.
4. Transfer to a food processor, and pulse until combined and a paste is formed.
5. Return the mixture to the skillet. Add the honey and lime juice and zest. Cook over low heat, reducing, for 15 minutes.
6. To use as a cook-in sauce, use half the sauce to cook 4 to 6 pieces of your chosen base, and save the rest to pour over when it's done cooking.
1. STORAGE: 1 to 2 weeks in the refrigerator, in a glass jar or plastic container

NUTRITION: Calories 17 Protein3 Fiber 1 Fats 4 Carbohydrates 11

88. Mojo Sauce

Preparation Time: 10 minutes

Cooking Time: 5minutes

Servings: 1 cup

INGREDIENTS:

- 3 garlic cloves, unpeeled
- Salt
- Freshly ground black pepper
- 2 tablespoons light oil (olive, grapeseed, vegetable, or avocado)
- 1 shallot, finely minced
- 1 green chile pepper (jalapeño or small Anaheim), finely minced
- ¾ cup sour orange juice (see Ingredient tip)
- SPECIAL EQUIPMENT NEEDED
- Mortar and pestle

DIRECTIONS:

1. In a small skillet over medium heat, dry roast the garlic cloves in their husks for 3 to 5 minutes. Let cool, peel, and finely mince them.
2. In the mortar, grind the garlic, and add pinch each of salt and pepper.
3. In a large bowl, combine the garlic with the oil, shallot, chile pepper, and orange juice. Whisk until the sauce comes together.
2. STORAGE: 5 days in the refrigerator in a glass jar or plastic container, or 2 months in the freezer in a plastic freezer bag or container
3. INGREDIENT TIP: Sour oranges can be hard to find; you can use ½ cup orange juice and 1 4 cup lime juice instead.

NUTRITION: Calories 17 Protein3 Fiber 1 Fats 4 Carbohydrates 11

89. Southwestern Squash Sauce

Preparation Time: 10 minutes

Cooking Time: 20 minutes

Servings: 3 cups

INGREDIENTS:

- 2 dried ancho chiles, stemmed and seeded
- 3 tablespoons extra-virgin olive oil
- 3 cups (1 pound) peeled, seeded, and cubed butternut squash
- 1 cup (1 4 pound) peeled and cubed beets
- 1 teaspoon ground allspice
- 2 shallots, diced
- 1 overripe banana, mashed
- 2 tablespoons unfiltered apple cider vinegar
- 2 teaspoons salt
- 1 fresh sage sprig, or about 4 to 5 leaves
- SPECIAL EQUIPMENT NEEDED
- Food processor

DIRECTIONS:

1. Soak the chiles in a small bowl of warm water for 20 minutes. Drain the water into a small bowl, and set aside the chiles and water separately.
2. In a large, deep pan or Dutch oven over medium heat, mix the oil with the squash, beets, and allspice. Cover and cook for 10 minutes, until the squash begins to soften.
3. Add the shallots, banana, and chiles, then mix in the vinegar. Cook for another 10 minutes over medium-low heat, until the shallots are translucent, stirring constantly.
4. Transfer to a food processor. Add the salt and sage, and pulse to desired consistency. Add some chili water (about ½ cup) to thin, if necessary.
1. STORAGE: 1 to 2 weeks in the refrigerator, in a glass jar or plastic container

2. REPURPOSING TIP: Add hot chicken or vegetable stock to the finished sauce to make this more of a soup.

NUTRITION: Calories 17 Protein3 Fiber 1 Fats 4 Carbohydrates 11

90. New Mexican Chili Sauce

Preparation Time: 10 minutes

Cooking Time: 20 minutes

Servings: 3 cups

INGREDIENTS:

- 7 or 8 New Mexico green chiles
- 1 tablespoon extra-virgin olive oil
- 2 cups cubed boneless pork, or protein of choice
- 1 medium onion, diced
- 3 or 4 garlic cloves, diced
- 3 tablespoons all-purpose flour
- 4 to 5 cups stock of choice, or water
- 2 teaspoons onion powder
- 2 teaspoons garlic powder
- 2 teaspoons salt

DIRECTIONS:

1. Preheat the oven to 350°F.
2. Spread the chiles on a baking sheet, and roast for 10 minutes. Or roast over a low flame on a grill for 15 to 20 minutes, flipping occasionally, until the skin is blackened. Place in a sealed container for 30 minutes while they cool. Then peel and dice.
3. In a large skillet over medium heat, cook the pork in the olive oil until browned, about 7 minutes. Add the onion and garlic, and cook until the onions are translucent, about 4 minutes. Add the chiles and cook for about 5 minutes, stirring often. Add the flour and cook, stirring constantly, to brown (but not burn!).
4. When the flour is browned and the protein is evenly coated, add the water, bring to a boil, and stir in the onion and garlic powders and salt. Cover and simmer on low for about 2 hours.
1. STORAGE: 4 days in the refrigerator, in a glass jar or plastic container, or a few months in the freezer in a plastic freezer bag or container
2. REPURPOSING TIP: Add this sauce to soups or stews to create a dynamic dish filled with spice and everything nice.

NUTRITION: Calories 17 Protein3 Fiber 1 Fats 4 Carbohydrates 11

91. <u>Everyday Barbecue Sauce</u>

Preparation Time: 15 minutes

Cooking Time: 10 minutes

Servings: 3

INGREDIENTS:

- 2 cups good-quality, raw, unfiltered apple cider vinegar
- 2 tablespoons tomato paste
- 2 tablespoons brown sugar
- 1 tablespoon kosher salt
- 1 tablespoon freshly ground black pepper
- 1 teaspoon garlic powder
- 1 teaspoon ground cayenne pepper
- ½ teaspoon ground allspice

DIRECTIONS:

1. In a jar with a lid, combine the vinegar, tomato paste, sugar, salt, black pepper, garlic powder, cayenne pepper, and allspice. Seal and shake vigorously until everything are evenly distributed.
2. Use immediately, or refrigerate. Shake before using.
1. STORAGE: 1 month in the refrigerator in a glass jar, or freeze in an ice cube tray and keep 3 months in the freezer in a freezer bag
2. REPURPOSING TIP: Liven up slaws and potato salad with a dash of this sauce, or use it as a marinade or baste while cooking.

NUTRITION: Calories 17 Protein3 Fiber 1 Fats 4 Carbohydrates 11

92. <u>Forest Berry Sauce</u>

Preparation Time: 15 minutes

Cooking Time: 10 minutes

Servings: 3

INGREDIENTS:

- 1 cup fresh huckleberries, stemmed and thoroughly washed (see Ingredient tip)
- ½ cup chopped fresh ramps (wild garlic; see Ingredient tip)
- ½ cup extra-virgin olive oil
- Salt
- Freshly ground black pepper
- SPECIAL EQUIPMENT NEEDED
- Blender or food processor

DIRECTIONS:

1. In a food processor or blender, combine the berries, ramps, and oil and blend into a paste. Add salt a pinch at a time until you taste the full profile of the berries. Sprinkle on pepper to taste.

2. Use this sauce on filets of salmon, halibut, trout, steak, or duck by smothering the entire top side of the protein with a thick layer of sauce, until the flesh is no longer visible.
3. Place the protein on a wood slab on a high-heat fire or grill.
4. The sauce should bubble just as the protein reaches ideal internal temperature (130° to 150°F for fish). Add more sauce as a baste if the protein needs more Cooking Time.
1. STORAGE: 1 week in the refrigerator, in a glass jar
2. INGREDIENT TIP: Fresh huckleberries are very easily found online and are often shipped overnight. You can substitute blueberries, or any forest fruit, for the huckleberries, but know that cultivated berries are generally sweeter than necessary for this kind of sauce. So, look for tart ones that don't over-sweeten the dish. Frozen ones are fine in this recipe; let them thaw to room temperature before using.
3. INGREDIENT TIP: If you can't find ramps, you can use the green part of spring onions, scallions, or a leek.

NUTRITION: Calories 17 Protein3 Fiber 1 Fats 4 Carbohydrates 11

93. Silky White Wine Sauce

Preparation Time: 15 minutes

Cooking Time: 10 minutes

Servings: 3

INGREDIENTS:

- 7 teaspoons butter, divided
- 1 shallot, diced
- 1 stalk fresh lemongrass, cut in 1-inch slices (optional; see Ingredient tip)
- 2 garlic cloves, whole
- 1 teaspoon white pepper
- 11 4 cups New Zealand Sauvignon Blanc
- 1½ teaspoons chopped fresh tarragon
- 1 tablespoon freshly squeezed lemon juice
- 1 teaspoon lemon zest
- ¾ cup heavy (whipping) cream
- Salt

DIRECTIONS:

1. In a medium saucepan over medium-low heat, heat 1 teaspoon of butter. Add the shallots and lemongrass (if using), and cook for 2 to 3 minutes.
2. Add the garlic, white pepper, wine, tarragon, and lemon juice and zest. Bring to a simmer over medium-high heat, and cook for 6 minutes.
3. Remove the strips of lemongrass and garlic cloves, and add the remaining 6 teaspoons of butter. Cook until it melts. Add the cream.
4. Turn the heat to low and let simmer for 10 minutes. Season with salt.
1. STORAGE: 1 week in the refrigerator, in a glass jar or plastic container

2. INGREDIENT TIP: To cut lemongrass, you must chop off the top and bottom and bisect the stalk to remove the tough outer layers, revealing the tender inside.

NUTRITION: Calories 17 Protein3 Fiber 1 Fats 4 Carbohydrates 11

94. Coconut Milk Sauce

Preparation Time: 15 minutes

Cooking Time: 10 minutes

Servings: 3

INGREDIENTS:

- 2 tablespoons vegetable oil
- 3 to 4 garlic cloves, minced
- 1-pound medium to large shrimp, heads removed, shelled and deveined, or your protein of choice
- 1 4 cup white vinegar (optional)
- 1 fourth teaspoon freshly ground black pepper
- 1 dried bay leaf
- 1 (13.5-ounce) can full-fat coconut milk, or 1 cup fresh (may be reduced to desired consistency)
- Fish sauce or salt, for seasoning
- 1 small jalapeño pepper, halved lengthwise, seeded, and sliced
- 1 tablespoon achiote oil (see Ingredient tip)
- 2 scallions, green parts only, chopped, for garnish

DIRECTIONS:

1. In a large pan over medium heat, heat the oil. Sauté the garlic until golden brown and aromatic, about 2 minutes.
2. Add the shrimp, followed by the vinegar (if using), without stirring. When the liquid stars to boil, sprinkle in the pepper and add the bay leaf.
3. Pour in the coconut milk. Cook for about 2 minutes, until it boils. Season with fish sauce.
4. Add the sliced jalapeño and achiote oil, and cook for another 3 to 4 minutes. Take care to not overcook the shrimp or they will become rubbery and tough. They should be light and flavorful.
5. Remove from the heat, and serve garnished with the scallions.
1. STORAGE: 2 weeks in the refrigerator, in a glass jar or plastic container
2. INGREDIENT TIP: Make achiote oil by frying 1 tablespoon annatto seeds in ½ cup peanut oil for about 3 or 4 minutes. Strain out the seeds. Annatto (also called achiote) can be found in most Latin markets or ordered online.

NUTRITION: Calories 17 Protein3 Fiber 1 Fats 4 Carbohydrates 11

95. Peanut Sauce

Preparation Time: 15 minutes

Cooking Time: 10 minutes

Servings: 3

INGREDIENTS:

- 11 4 cups water
- 7 tablespoons seedless tamarind pulp
- ½ cup raw peanuts
- 1 tablespoon extra-virgin olive oil or peanut oil
- 1 to 2 tablespoons Thai red curry paste (see Ingredient tip)
- 4 tablespoons messman curry paste (see Ingredient tip)
  - o   ounces full-fat coconut milk
- 1 to 2 tablespoons liquid coconut sugar
- Pinch salt
- ½ teaspoon fish sauce
- SPECIAL EQUIPMENT NEEDED
- Mortar and pestle

DIRECTIONS:

1. In a small saucepan, boil the water. Take the pan off the heat, and add the tamarind pulp, stir until mixed, remove from the heat, and let sit for 30 minutes. Squeeze through a sieve to remove any pulp or plant mass. Save what you don't use for future use (like in Nam Jim).

2. In a dry, medium pan over low heat, roast the peanuts until slightly charred (not burned), about 10 minutes. Place in the mortar with the oil, and work the peanuts into a chunky paste. This takes a little while but is worth the effort.

3. In a nonstick medium pot over medium heat, slightly sauté the red curry and messman curry pastes, continuously stirring with a wooden spoon, for about 1 minute.

4. Slowly add some of the coconut milk into the pot, and continue to stir until the liquid evaporates. Then add a little more coconut milk and continue to stir the mixture for 3 to 4 minutes more.

5. Add the rest of the coconut milk and the peanut paste, coconut sugar, and 2 to 3 tablespoons of the liquid tamarind pulp. Continue to stir and allow the sauce to bubble and thicken. Add a pinch of salt, stir, then add the fish sauce to taste. Let cool.

1. STORAGE: 1 week in the refrigerator, in a glass jar

2. INGREDIENT TIP: You can find both messman and red curry paste in Asian grocery stores or online in small jars or cans.

NUTRITION: Calories 17 Protein3 Fiber 1 Fats 4

96. <u>Carbohydrates 11</u>

Sweet And Sour Sauce

Preparation Time: 15 minutes

Cooking Time: 10 minutes

Servings: 3

INGREDIENTS:

- Aminos instead of fish sauce.
- FOR THE TAMARIND SAUCE
- 11 4 cups water
- 7 tablespoons seedless tamarind pulp
- 1 4 cup fish sauce
- 1 4 cup granulated palm sugar
- 2 tablespoons white vinegar
- 2 tablespoons superfine or caster sugar
- FOR NAM JIM
- 2 tablespoons dried serrano chiles (or chiles of choice) soaked in warm water for 30 minutes and drained
- 1 tablespoon minced garlic
- 1 tablespoon chopped shallot
- 1 tablespoon chopped coriander root (or chopped fresh cilantro stalk and 1 teaspoon ground cumin; see Ingredient tip)
- 1 tablespoon chopped onion
- 1½ tablespoons vegetable oil
- Salt
- SPECIAL EQUIPMENT NEEDED
- Blender or food processor

- TO MAKE THE TAMARIND SAUCE

DIRECTIONS:

1. In a small saucepan, boil the water. Take the pan off the heat, and add the tamarind pulp. Remove from the heat, let sit for 30 minutes, and stir until mixed. Squeeze through a sieve to remove any pulp or plant mass. You should end up with just over ¾ cups liquid concentrate. Add a bit more water if necessary.
2. Heat a wok or large skillet over high heat. Add your tamarind concentrate, and bring to a boil. Add the fish sauce and then the palm sugar.
3. When everything is dissolved, add the vinegar and caster sugar. Turn the heat to low and cook for 5 minutes, until the tamarind sauce is thick and syrupy. Set aside.
4. TO MAKE THE NAM JIM
5. In the food processor, blend the chiles, garlic, shallot, coriander root, onion, and 3 tablespoons of your tamarind sauce until you have a paste.
6. In a small skillet over medium heat, heat the oil. Add the paste, and bring to a simmering boil. Stir to combine.
7. Lower the heat. Add the remainder of the tamarind sauce, and season with salt. Remove from the heat and let cool.

NUTRITION: Calories 17 Protein3 Fiber 1 Fats 4 Carbohydrates 11

97. Lemongrass Curry

Preparation Time: 15 minutes

Cooking Time: 10 minutes

Servings: 3

INGREDIENTS:

- 2 dried chiles
- 2 fresh lemongrass stalks (cores only), sliced into rounds
- 1 teaspoon fish sauce
- 6 garlic cloves, crushed
- 10 kaffir lime leaves, deveined (see Ingredient tip)
- 2 tablespoons vegetable oil, divided
- 2 shallots, diced
- 1 (13.5-ounce) can full-fat coconut milk
- 2 whole star anise pods
- 1 teaspoon ground turmeric or 1-inch piece fresh, minced
- 1 teaspoon dried galangal or 1-inch piece fresh, minced (see Ingredient tip)
- 1 teaspoon granulated palm sugar or sweetened condensed milk
- Salt
- SPECIAL EQUIPMENT NEEDED
- Food processor

DIRECTIONS:

1. Let the chiles soak in a small bowl of warm water for 20 minutes to reconstitute while you prepare the other ingredients. Drain well, then remove the seeds and stems.
2. In the food processor, grind together the lemongrass, fish sauce, garlic, lime leaves, chiles, and 1 tablespoon of oil to make the kroeung paste.
3. In a medium saucepan over low heat, heat the remaining 1 tablespoon of oil. Add the shallots and cook until slightly translucent, 2 minutes or so. Add the kroeung paste and simmer for 2 to 3 minutes, until it slightly browns.
4. Add the coconut milk, star anise, turmeric, galangal, and sugar, and stir. Let simmer for 10 minutes, or until the coconut milk is smooth. Season with salt.
5. STORAGE: 4 to 5 days in the refrigerator, in a glass jar or plastic container
6. INGREDIENT TIP: Galangal is a cousin of ginger and can be ordered dried on the Internet. Though not ideal, you can substitute lime zest and a squeeze of lemon juice for kaffir lime leaves.
7. REPURPOSING TIP: There is a lot of room to play with taste and color. Add more basic chili paste and leave out the turmeric for more of a red kroeung. Cook your protein of choice in the sauce by adding it at the end of step 3, and simmer until cooked through.

NUTRITION: Calories 17 Protein3 Fiber 1 Fats 4 Carbohydrates 11

98. Dipping Fish Sauce

Preparation Time: 15 minutes

Cooking Time: 10 minutes

Servings: 3

INGREDIENTS:

- 2 whole garlic cloves
- 1 to 3 bird's eye chiles, fresh or frozen
- 1 4 cup sugar
- 1 4 cup fish sauce
- 1 4 cups freshly squeezed lime juice
- SPECIAL EQUIPMENT NEEDED
- Mortar and pestle (or chef's knife)

DIRECTIONS:

1. In the mortar and pestle, crush the garlic and chiles until they form a paste. Or crush the ingredients with the side of a chef's knife. You can add some of the sugar to help you achieve the paste consistency.
2. Transfer to a small bowl. Add the rest of the sugar, and mix very well.
3. Add the fish sauce and lime juice, and stir until the sugar is dissolved.
4. STORAGE: 1 to 2 weeks, in a glass jar or plastic container

NUTRITION: Calories 17 Protein3 Fiber 1 Fats 4 Carbohydrates 11

99. Apple Sauce Treat

Preparation Time: ten minutes

Cooking Time: 0 minutes

Servings: 1

INGREDIENTS:

- ½ teaspoon cinnamon
- 1 ½ teaspoons toasted slivered almonds
- 1 4 cup low Fat cottage cheese
- 1 4 cup unsweetened applesauce

DIRECTIONS:

1. Combine the cottage cheese and applesauce in a container, stirring well.
2. Drizzle with cinnamon and mix thoroughly.
3. Drizzle the top with almonds, pick up your spoon, and enjoy.

NUTRITION: Calories: 225 kcal Protein: 16.24 g Fat: 14.17 g Carbohydrates: 8.54 g

100. Avocado And Egg Sandwich

Preparation Time: ten minutes

Cooking Time: 0 minutes

Servings: 2

INGREDIENTS:

- ½ lime juice
- 1 avocado (ripe)
- 1 egg, organic
- 1 scallion
- 2 radishes
- 2 slices of who wheat, seed bread
- A pinch of salt (sea or Himalayan)
- Black pepper – to your taste
- Mixed seeds – to your choice

DIRECTIONS:

1. Peel the avocado.
2. Boil the egg (soft boiled).
3. Chop the radishes to thin slices.
4. Dice the scallion (finely).
5. Mix avocado, salt, and lime juice in a container. Mash the mixture meticulously.
6. Spread the mixture onto the bread.
7. Put in some radish.
8. Put tender boiled eggs on top.

9. Put in some scallion, seeds, and pepper.

NUTRITION: Calories: 342 kcal Protein: 12.36 g Fat: 22.99 g Carbohydrates: 26.54 g

101. Tahini Dip

Preparation Time: ten minutes

Cooking Time: 0 minutes

Servings: 2-4

INGREDIENTS:

- 1 fourth cup of tahini
- ½ tsp of maple syrup
- 1 small grated or thoroughly minced clove of garlic (this is optional)
- 1 tbsp. of apple cider vinegar
- 1 tbsp. of freshly squeezed lemon juice
- 1 tbsp. of tamari
- 1 tsp of finely grated ginger, or ½ tsp of ground ginger
- 1 tsp of turmeric
- 1 third cup of water

DIRECTIONS:

1. Blend or whisk all ingredients together. Place the dressing in an airtight container then place in your fridge for approximately 5 days.
2. Enjoy!

NUTRITION: Calories: 120 kcal Protein: 4.77 g Fat: 9.63 g Carbohydrates: 5.12 g

102. Homemade Ginger Dressing

Preparation Time: ten minutes

Cooking Time: 0 minutes

Servings: 2-4

INGREDIENTS:

- 1 fourth cup of chopped celery
- 1 fourth cup of honey or maple syrup
- 1 fourth cup of water
- ½ cup of chopped carrots
- ½ tsp of white pepper
- 1 cup of chopped onion
- 1 cup of extra-virgin olive oil
- 1 tsp of freshly minced garlic
- 1 tsp of kosher salt
- 2 ½ tbsp. of unsalted, gluten-free soy sauce

- 2 tbsp. of ketchup
- 2 3 cup of rice vinegar
- 6 tbsp. of freshly grated ginger

DIRECTIONS:

1. Put the onion, ginger, celery, carrots, and garlic into a blender. Blend until the mixture are fine but still lumpy from the small vegetable chunks.
2. Put in in the vinegar, water, ketchup, soy sauce, honey or maple syrup, lemon juice, salt, and pepper. Pulse until the ingredients are well blended.
3. Slowly put in the oil while blending, until everything is thoroughly combined. The mixture must be runny but still grainy.
4. Serve with a winter salad.

NUTRITION: Calories: 389 kcal Protein: 2.71 g Fat: 32.08 g Carbohydrates: 22.14 g

103. Homemade Lemon Vinaigrette

Preparation Time: ten minutes

Cooking Time: 0 minutes

Servings: 2-4

INGREDIENTS:

- 1 4 tsp of sea salt
- ½ tsp of Dijon mustard, without preservatives
- ½ tsp of lemon zest
- 1 tsp of honey or maple syrup
- 2 tbsp. of freshly squeezed lemon juice
- 3 tbsp. of extra-virgin olive oil
- Freshly ground black pepper

DIRECTIONS:

1. Whisk all together the ingredients apart from olive oil and black pepper in a small container. Then progressively put in 3 tbsp. of olive oil while continuously whisking until well blended. Put in some ground black pepper to taste.
2. Put mason jar and place in your fridge for maximum 3 days.
3. Serve with a garden salad.

NUTRITION: Calories: 68 kcal Protein: 1.69 g Fat: 6.06 g Carbohydrates: 1.71 g

104. Homemade Ranch

Preparation Time: ten minutes

Cooking Time: 0 minutes

Servings: 2-4

INGREDIENTS:

- 1 fourth cup of Greek yogurt

- 1 4 tsp Kosher salt
- ½ cup of natural mayonnaise, without preservatives
- ½ tsp of dried dill
- ½ tsp of dried parsley
- ½ tsp of garlic powder
- ½ tsp of onion powder
- ¾ cup of non-dairy milk
- 1 8 tsp Freshly ground black pepper
- 2 tsp of dried chives

DIRECTIONS:

1. Combine all ingredients apart from the milk into a medium container. Mix together until well blended.
2. Put in in the milk and mix thoroughly.
3. Pour in a mason jar or an airtight container. Serve instantly or place in your fridge for maximum 2 hours to keep the freshness. Put in your refrigerator for maximum 5 days.
4. Serve with a garden or fruit salad.

NUTRITION: Calories: 482 kcal Protein: 3.55 g Fat: 51.98 g Carbohydrates: 1.63 g

105. Honey Bean Dip

Preparation Time: five minutes

Cooking Time: 0 minutes

Servings: 3-4

INGREDIENTS:

- 1 4 teaspoon ground cumin
- 1 4 teaspoon salt
- 1 (14-ounce) can each of kidney beans and black beans
- 1 tablespoon apple cider vinegar
- 1 teaspoon lime juice
- 2 cherry tomatoes
- 2 garlic cloves
- 2 tablespoons filtered water
- 2 teaspoons raw honey
- Freshly ground black pepper to taste
- Pinch cayenne pepper to taste

DIRECTIONS:

1. In a blender or food processor, put together the beans, garlic, tomatoes, water, vinegar, honey, lime juice, cumin, salt, cayenne pepper, and black pepper.
2. Blend until it becomes smooth. Put in the mix in a container.
3. Cover and place in your fridge to chill. You can place in your fridge for maximum 5 days.

NUTRITION: Calories 158 Fat: 1g Carbohydrates: 33g Fiber: 8g Protein: 9g

106. Soy With Honey And Ginger Glaze

Preparation Time: ten minutes

Cooking Time: 0 minutes

Servings: 2-4

INGREDIENTS:

- 1 fourth cup of honey
- 1 tbsp. of rice vinegar
- 1 tsp of freshly grated ginger
- 2 tbsp. gluten-free soy sauce

DIRECTIONS:

1. Put all together the ingredients into a small container and whisk well.
2. Serve with a vegetables, chickens, or seafood.
3. Keep the glaze in a mason jar, firmly covered, and place in your fridge for maximum four days.

NUTRITION: Calories: 90 kcal Protein: 2.32 g Fat: 1.54 g Carbohydrates: 17.99 g

107. Cucumber And Dill Sauce

Preparation Time: ten minutes

Cooking Time: 0 minutes

Servings: 2-4

INGREDIENTS:

- 1 4 cup of lemon juice
- 1 cucumber, peeled and squeezed to remove surplus liquid
- 1 cup of freshly chopped dill
- 1 tsp of sea salt
- 450g of Greek yogurt

DIRECTIONS:

1. In a moderate-sized container, put together the yogurt, cucumber, and dill then stir until well blended. Put in in the lemon juice and salt to taste.
2. Cover and place in your fridge for approximately 1-2 hours before you serve to keep its freshness. Best serve with Mediterranean food, chips, fish, or even bread.

NUTRITION: Calories: 97 kcal Protein: 13.49 g Fat: 2.1 g Carbohydrates: 6.34 g

108. Dairy-Free Creamy Turmeric Dressing

Preparation Time: ten minutes

Cooking Time: 0 minutes

Servings: 2-4

INGREDIENTS:

- ½ cup of extra-virgin olive oil
- ½ cup of tahini
- 1 tbsp. of turmeric powder
- 2 tbsp. of lemon juice
- 2 tsp of honey
- Some sea salt and pepper

DIRECTIONS:

1. In a container, whisk all ingredients until well blended.
2. Store in a mason jar and place in your fridge for maximum 5 days.

NUTRITION: Calories: 328 kcal Protein: 7.3 g Fat: 29.36 g Carbohydrates: 12.43 g

109. Herby Raita

Preparation Time: ten minutes

Cooking Time: 0 minutes

Servings: 2-4

INGREDIENTS:

- 1 fourth cup of freshly chopped mint
- 1 4 tsp of freshly ground black pepper
- ½ tsp of sea salt
- 1 cup of Greek yogurt
- 1 large-sized cucumber, shredded
- 1 tsp of lemon juice

DIRECTIONS:

1. Combine the cucumber with 1 4 tsp of salt in a sieve and leave to drain for fifteen minutes. Shake to release any surplus liquid and move to a kitchen towel. Squeeze out as much liquid as you can using the paper towel.
2. Put the cucumber into a medium container then mix in the rest of the ingredients until well blended.
3. Put in your fridge for minimum 2 hours to keep its freshness. Best consume with spicy foods as it could relief the spiciness.

NUTRITION: Calories: 69 kcal Protein: 4.33 g Fat: 3.66 g Carbohydrates: 4.93 g

110. Creamy Avocado Dressing

Preparation Time: ten minutes

Cooking Time: 0 minutes

Servings: 2-4

INGREDIENTS:

- ½ cup of extra-virgin olive oil
- 1 clove of garlic, chopped
- 1 tsp of honey or maple syrup
- 2 small or 1 large-sized avocado, pitted and chopped
- 2 tsp of lemon or lime juice
- 3 tbsp. of chopped parsley
- 3 tbsp. of red wine vinegar
- Onion powder
- Some Kosher salt and ground black pepper

DIRECTIONS:

1. Combine all ingredients into a blender, apart from the oil. As the ingredients are mixed, progressively put in the oil into the mixture. Blend until the desired smoothness is achieved or becomes liquid.
2. Use as a vegetable or fruit salad dressing. Put in your fridge for maximum 5 days.

NUTRITION: Calories: 300 kcal Protein: 4.09 g Fat: 27.9 g Carbohydrates: 11.41 g

111. Creamy Homemade Greek Dressing

Preparation Time: ten minutes

Cooking Time: 0 minutes

Servings: 2-4

INGREDIENTS:

- 1 4 cup non-dairy milk (e.g., almond, rice milk)
- ½ cup of high-quality mayonnaise, without preservatives
- ½ tsp dried basil
- ½ tsp dried oregano
- ½ tsp parsley
- ½ tsp thyme
- 1 3 cup of extra-virgin olive oil
- 1 4 cup of white wine vinegar
- 2 cloves of garlic, minced
- 2 tbsp. of lemon or lime juice
- 2 tsp of honey
- A few tablespoons of water
- Some Kosher salt and pepper

DIRECTIONS:

1. Put all together ingredients in a mason jar and shake, cover firmly, and shake thoroughly. Place in your fridge for a few hours before you serve or serve instantly on your favorite vegetable or fruit salad.
2. Shake well before use. Put in your fridge for maximum 5 days.
3. You may put in a few tablespoons of water to tune the consistency as per your preference.

NUTRITION: Calories: 474 kcal Protein: 2.08 g Fat: 50.1 g Carbohydrates: 5.31 g

112. Bean Potato Spread

Preparation Time: twenty-five minutes

Cooking Time: 0 minutes

Servings: 7-8

INGREDIENTS:

- 1 4 cup sesame paste
- ½ teaspoon cumin, ground
- 1 cup garbanzo beans, drained and washed
- 1 tablespoon olive oil
- 2 tablespoons lime juice
- 2 tablespoons water
- 4 cups cooked sweet potatoes, peeled and chopped
- 5 garlic cloves, minced

- A pinch of salt

DIRECTIONS:
1. Throw all the ingredients into a blender and blend to make a smooth mix.
2. Move to a container.
3. Serve with carrot, celery, or veggie sticks.

NUTRITION: Calories 156 Fat: 3g Carbohydrates: 10g Fiber: 6g Protein: 8g

113. Cashew Ginger Dip

Preparation Time: five minutes

Cooking Time: 0 minutes

Servings: 1

INGREDIENTS:
- 1 4 cup filtered water
- 1 4 teaspoon salt
- ½ teaspoon ground ginger
- 1 cup cashews, soaked in water for about twenty minutes and drained
- 1 tablespoon extra-virgin olive oil
- 1 teaspoon lemon juice
- 2 garlic cloves
- 2 teaspoons coconut aminos
- Pinch cayenne pepper

DIRECTIONS:
1. In a blender or food processor, put together the cashews, garlic, water, olive oil, aminos, lemon juice, ginger, salt, and cayenne pepper.
2. Put in the mix in a container.
3. Cover and place in your fridge until chilled. You can use store it for 4-5 days in your fridge.

NUTRITION: Calories 124 Fat: 9g Carbohydrates: 5g Fiber: 1g Protein: 3g

114. Almond Pear Express Cream

INGREDIENTS
- 1 pot of semi-skimmed milk cheese with 3% fat
- 1 teaspoon of almond powder
- 1 half teaspoon of flax seeds
- 2 drops of bitter almond extract
- 1 teaspoon of honey
- 1 lemon
- 1 pear
- 1 small square of dark chocolate

DIRECTION:

1. Place the flax seeds in a non-stick pan. Roast them for 2 minutes over medium heat, stirring them, so they do not burn.
2. Wash the lemon under running water, sponge it, and squeeze it.
3. Mix the white cheese with almond powder, bitter almond extract, 2 teaspoons lemon juice, honey, and flax seeds.
4. Wash the pear, peel it, dice it, and lemon it. Mix with almond cream.
5. Slice the chocolate into thin chips and sprinkle the cream. Enjoy it immediately.

115. Red Pepper Chickpea Dip

Preparation Time: 10 minutes

Cooking Time: 0 minutes

Servings: 6

INGREDIENTS:

- 1 3 c. tahini (sesame seed paste)
- 2 T. fresh lemon juice
- salt and black pepper, to taste
- 1 (15 oz.) can chickpeas, rinsed and drained
- 1 4 c. roasted red bell peppers, (if bottled, rinse, drain, and chopped)
- 2 cloves garlic, minced
- 1 4 c. olive oil

DIRECTIONS:

1. All the ingredients must be put in a blender or food processor then pulsed until smooth. Taste and adjust seasonings with salt and pepper.

NUTRITION: Calories 164 Fat: 4.7g Fiber: 7.9g Carbs: 29.4g Protein: 4.1g

116. Baked Fennel

Preparation Time: 5 minutes

Cooking Time: 8 minutes

Servings: 2

INGREDIENTS:

- 1 large fennel bulb, fronds removed and reserved, sliced
- 2 teaspoons olive oil
- 1 4 teaspoon salt
- 2 lemon wedges
- 1 tablespoon chopped fennel fronds

DIRECTIONS:

1. Preheat air fryer at 350°F for 3 minutes.
2. Brush fennel slices on both sides with olive oil and season with salt.
3. Place fennel slices in ungreased air fryer basket. Cook 8 minutes.
4. Transfer to a medium serving dish. Squeeze lemon on fennel and garnish with chopped fronds. Serve warm.

NUTRITION: Calories: 78 Protein: 2g Fiber: 4g Net carbohydrates: 5g Fat: 5g Sodium: 353mg
Carbohydrates: 9g Sugar: 5g

117. Madeira Cake

Preparation Time: 15 minutes

Cooking Time: 10 minutes

Servings: 6-8

INGREDIENTS:

- 175g (6oz) caster sugar
- 250g (9oz) self-rising flour
- 175g (6oz) unsalted butter, at room temperature
- Three eggs
- One lemon, zest only
- 2-3 tbsp milk

DIRECTIONS:

1. Pre-heat oven to 180°C 350°F Gas 4.
2. Grease an 18cm round cake tin, line the base with greaseproof paper and grease it
3. Cream the sugar and butter together in a bowl until fluffy and pale.
4. Beat in the eggs, one at a time and add a tablespoon of the flour with the last egg to prevent the mixture curdling.
5. Sieve the flour and gently fold in, with milk to give a mixture that falls from the spoon. Fold in the lemon zest.
6. Spoon the mixture into the prepared tin and level the top lightly. Bake on the middle shelf of the oven until golden-brown on top and a skewer inserted into the center comes out clean.

NUTRITION: Calories 117 Protein 13 Fiber 3 Fats 32 Carbohydrates 1151

118. Lemon Cheesecake

Preparation Time: 15 minutes

Cooking Time: 40 minutes

Servings: 6

INGREDIENTS:

- 100g (3½oz) soft unsalted butter
- 200g (7oz) digestive biscuits
- For the topping
- One packet cream cheese (a standard packet typically around 200-300g)
- 250g (9oz) icing sugar (sifted)
- One tub single cream (or whipping cream)
- Juice of One lemon

DIRECTIONS:

1. Whizz the biscuits in a food processor until you have fine crumbs, add the butter through the nozzle in tiny chunks while the processor is still working. You should have a damp dough-like consistency.
2. Butter a tin and press the bottom mixture hard into the bottom of the tin and place it in the refrigerator to set.
3. Beat the cream until it is thickened enough to almost retain its shape. Use an electric whisk if you have one to enable you save time
4. Beat in the packet of cream cheese until the mixture is smooth.
5. Add the sifted lemon juice and icing sugar and beat again a smooth thick consistency is achieved.
6. Pour the topping on the base and spread, put the tin back in the refrigerator until the topping is set. Add fruit as preferred.

NUTRITION: Calories 117 Protein 13 Fiber 3 Fats 32 Carbohydrates 115

119. Easy Fish Cakes

Preparation Time: 15 minutes

Cooking Time: 20 minutes

Servings: 3

INGREDIENTS:

- Two medium potatoes (or sweet potatoes)
- freshly ground black pepper
- 200g (7oz) cooked flaked fish, either a tin of tuna or salmon, or smoked mackerel
- a small lemon juice only
- One tbsp of olive oil or vegetable
- 100g(3½oz) cream crackers or similar savory biscuits (or breadcrumbs if you have them)
- Optional extras
- One tablespoon chopped chives or parsley
- Two spring onions, chopped
- One tsp wholegrain mustard
- One tablespoon grated cheddar

DIRECTIONS:

1. Preheat oven to 220°C (200°C Fan) Gas 7 425°F.

2. Peel and then boil the potatoes. After twenty - thirty minutes the potatoes should feel soft if not, cook them for a few more minutes, then rinse and leave them to cool.

3. Mash the potato with a masher, clean fingers or fork or.

4. Add the fish and blend thoroughly. Add the lemon, a small amount of pepper and some of the optional extras you like. Have a taste: you can decide to add more lemon or pepper.

5. In a sandwich bag, put the crackers and wrap them in a layers of kitchen paper or clean tea towel. Using a rolling pin, crush the crackers. Pour the cracker crumbs in a plate.

6. Wet your hands a bit and roll the fishcake mixture into tiny balls. You can flatten them into patties, so don't think too much about making perfect balls. You want a thin coating of crumbs all over the fishcakes to make the outside of the fishcakes moist again and drive them into the bowl of crushed crackers.

7. Place the fish cakes on top and pour the oil over the bottom of a baking tray. Turn them all over once, so that each side has a little oil on it.

8. Bake the fishcakes on one side for ten minutes and then turn the fishcakes over for another ten minutes before putting them back in the oven or until the fishcakes are golden brown. Remove from the oven carefully and leave to cool before serving.

NUTRITION: Calories 117 Protein 13 Fiber 3 Fats 32 Carbohydrates 115

120. Chocolate Pear Charlotte

Preparation Time: 15 minutes

Cooking Time: 30 minutes

Servings: 6

INGREDIENTS:

18 biscuits with a spoon

- 1 tablespoon liquid vanilla extract
- 2 beautiful ripe pears
- 2 jars of chocolate cream-dessert (250 g)
- 1 lemon
- 1 tablespoon chocolate granules

DIRECTION:

1. Wash the lemon under running water, sponge it, and squeeze it.

2. Wash the pears, peel them, and remove any excessively ripe parts. Cut them into cubes. Place them in a small saucepan with the lemon juice. Cook them covered over low heat for 20 minutes. At the end of cooking, crush them in the sauce.

3. Mix the vanilla extract with 4 tablespoons of water. Dip the biscuits very quickly in the vanilla and line the bottom and edges of 4 ramekins. Spread half of the cooled compote on the biscuits. Pour over the chocolate cream (a 1 2 pot per ramekin). Finish with the remaining compote. Place the charlottes in the refrigerator for at least 4 hours.

4. Unmold the charlottes just before serving and decorate them with chocolate granules.

5. Nutritional fact

6. The charlotte pear chocolate is dessert or energetic snack rich in carbohydrates. Thanks to the pears, it has good fiber and potassium content.

NUTRITION: Calories 117 Protein 13 Fiber 3 Fats 12 Carbohydrates 115

121. Peach Fondant

Preparation Time: 15 minutes

Cooking Time: 30 minutes

Servings: 6

INGREDIENTS:

- 2 pears Conference
- 2 eggs
- 1 fourth liters of semi-skimmed milk
- 2 tablespoons maple syrup or 3 teaspoons of sugar
- 1 lemon
- 30 g oat flakes
- 1 vanilla pod
- 2 tablespoons rum
- 2 level tablespoons of flaked almonds

DIRECTION:

1. Spread the vanilla pod under the water, then slice it in half and place it with the milk in a saucepan. Heat to a boil, then turn off the heat and let the vanilla brew.
2. Preheat the oven to 180 ° C.
3. Mix the oatmeal. Remove the vanilla pod from cooled milk and gradually mix milk and oatmeal. Add the maple syrup, the rum, then the 2 beaten egg omelet.
4. Wash the lemon and squeeze it. Wash the pears, cut them in half, remove the fibrous central part and the pips, peel them. Lemon them immediately to avoid blackening them. Arrange the 4 half-pears in a gratin dish. Pour over the milk mixture.
5. Bake for 30 minutes at 180 ° C. Check the cooking with a knife tip.
6. Quickly brown the flaked almonds in a non-stick frying pan and decorate the fondant.

NUTRITION: Calories 117 Protein 13 Fiber 3 Fats 32 Carbohydrates 115

122. Lemon Tassies

Preparation Time: 40 minutes

Cooking Time: 35-40 minutes

Servings: 12-14

INGREDIENTS:

- 8 oz. cream cheese, softened
- 1 cup unsalted butter, softened
- 2 1 2 cups all-purpose flour

94

- 4 eggs
- 1 3 cup fresh lemon juice
- 1 cup granulated sugar
- 1 3 cup melted unsalted butter
- 1 tsp. coconut extract
- 1 cup toasted sweetened flaked coconut

DIRECTIONS:

1. The crust is imperative to great tassies. Do not over mix the crust once you add the all-purpose flour. Work the dough gently.
2. Add the cream cheese and 1 cup softened butter to a mixing bowl. Using a mixer on medium speed, beat for 2 minutes or until well combined. Add the all-purpose flour and mix only until combined. Cover the bowl and refrigerate the dough for 1 hour or until the dough is well chilled.
3. Remove the dough from the refrigerator. Divide the dough into 48 equal pieces. Press each piece into two 24 count miniature muffin tins to form a crust. Preheat the oven to 350°. In a mixing bowl, add the eggs, lemon juice, granulated sugar, 1 3 cup melted butter and coconut extract. Whisk until well combined.
4. Pour the filling into the crust filling them almost to the top. Bake for 18-20 minutes or until the filling is set. Remove the pans from the oven and cool the tassies in the pans for 10 minutes. Remove the tassies from the pans and cool completely. Sprinkle the toasted coconut over the top before serving.

NUTRITION: Calories 121 Fat: 5.7h Fiber: 1.8g Carbs: 19.5g Protein: 4.1g

123. Number 0 Crab Cakes

Preparation Time: 1 hr. and 20 minutes

Cooking Time: 15-20 minutes

Servings: 6

INGREDIENTS:

- 1-pound crab meat lump or
- 1 tsp lemon juice
- claw
- 2 tsp prepared mustard
- 1 cup bread crumbs
- 2 tbsp. chopped parsley
- 1 egg
- 1 4 tsp red pepper or cayenne
- Hot sauce or Tabasco to taste
- 1 4 tsp black pepper
- 3 tbsp. mayonnaise
- 2 dashes Tabasco sauce
- 1 tsp Cajun seasoning

- 1 4 tsp onion powder
- 1 tbsp. Worcestershire sauce
- Butter for sautéing
- 1 4 tsp dry mustard

DIRECTIONS:

1. In a bowl or container, mix in all the ingredients but not the bread crumbs, butter and crab meat. Mix well then slowly put in the crab meat and breadcrumbs. Shape them into patties then chill before cooking. Once ready, heat butter and cook until each side is light brown.

NUTRITION: Calories 175 Fat: 8.4g Fiber: 5.4g Carbs: 16.4g Protein: 9.4g

DANG GOOD DRINKS AND COCKTAILS

124. Raspberries For Recovery

Preparation Time: 15 minutes

Cooking Time: 5 minutes

Servings: 2

INGREDIENTS:

- 11 2 cups raspberries
- 1 tablespoon lemon juice
- 1 cup nonfat Greek yogurt
- 1 tablespoon ground flax seed
- 1 teaspoon organic honey

DIRECTIONS:

1. In the 18-ounce NutriBullet cup, combine all ingredients.
2. Blend until all ingredients are thoroughly liquefied and combined, 30–60 seconds.
3. Consume immediately, or store with an airtight lid in the refrigerator for no more than 3–4 hours.

NUTRITION: Calories: 167 Fat: 4 g Protein: 9 g Sodium: 5 mg Fiber: 12 g Carbohydrates: 29 g Sugar: 14 g

125. Tomato Fresca Cooler

Preparation Time: 20 minutes plus chilling time

Cooking Time: 30 minutes

Servings: 8-10

INGREDIENTS:

- 10 cups chopped fresh tomato
- 1 2 cup water
- 1 4 cup chopped green bell pepper
- 1 4 cup chopped carrot
- 1 4 cup chopped celery
- 1 4 cup fresh lemon juice
- 2 tbs. chopped onion
- 1 tbs. salt
- 1 small serrano pepper, seeded and diced

DIRECTIONS:

1. In a pot add in all the ingredients. Stir until well combined and bring the juice to a boil. Reduce the heat to low. Place a lid on the pan and simmer the juice for 30 minutes. Remove the pan from the heat and cool the juice completely.
2. Unless you have a large blender, you will have to puree the juice in batches. Add the juice to a blender and puree until smooth. Pour into a pitcher and chill before serving.
3. You do not have to cook the juice if wanting raw juice. Process in a blender as directed above. I prefer the cooked juice as the acidity level is decreased.

NUTRITION: Calories:10 Fat: 1.4g Fiber: 10.5g Carbs: 5g Protein: 1.5.g

126. Holiday Punch

Preparation Time: 10 minutes

Cooking Time: 0 minutes

Servings: 8

INGREDIENTS:

- 20 ounces fresh orange juice
- 12 ounces canned or bottled pineapple juice
- 8 ounces good bourbon
- 2 ounces lime juice
- 2 ounces Grenadine
- 2 tbsp light brown sugar
- 16 ounces carbonated lemon-lime soda

DIRECTIONS:

1. Combine all ingredients in a large pitcher and stir to dissolve the sugar. Cover and refrigerate until ready to serve. To serve, rim tall glasses with lime juice and twist in raw sugar. Fill glasses with shaved ice and pour punch over ice. Garnish with lime and orange slices, and stemmed maraschino cherries.

NUTRITION: Calories 101 Fat: 1.4g Fiber: 2.9g Carbs: 5g Protein: 0.45.g

127. Southern Almond Tea

Preparation Time: 10 minutes

Cooking Time: 5 minutes

Servings: 4

INGREDIENTS:

- 4 regular-sized tea bags or 1 family-sized tea bag
- 2 cups boiling water
- 3 4 to 1 cup sugar
- 1 3 cup lemon juice
- 1 t vanilla extract
- 1 t almond extract
- 2 quarts water

DIRECTIONS:

1. Make the tea, and steep for 5 minutes.
2. Add the sugar, juice, flavorings, and the 2 quarts of water.
3. Chill thoroughly, and serve over ice.

NUTRITION: Calories 21 Fat: 0.1g Fiber: 0.5g Carbs: 1.5g Protein: 0.1g

128. Southern Lemon Iced Tea

Preparation Time: 15 minutes plus chilling time

Cooking Time: 15 minutes

Servings: 7

INGREDIENTS:

- 7 cups cold water
- 2 family size tea bags
- 1 cup fresh mint leaves
- 1 2 cup granulated sugar
- 6 oz. can freeze lemonade concentrate, thawed

DIRECTIONS:

1. In a small sauce pan over medium heat, add 3 cups water. Bring the water to a boil and remove the pan from the heat. Add the tea bags and mint leaves to the pan. Place a lid on the pan and steep the tea for 10 minutes. Remove the tea bags and mint from the pan and discard.
2. Add the granulated sugar to the tea. Stir until the sugar dissolves. Pour the tea into a 3-quart pitcher. Add the lemonade concentrate and 4 cups water. Stir until combined. Chill the tea for 4 hours before serving for best taste. Serve the tea over ice and with lemon slices if desired.

NUTRITION: Calories 01 Fat: 1.4 Fiber: 0.9g Carbs: 5g Protein: 0.5g

129. FIVE BONUS Mnt Dew Drink Recipes!

Agent Orange #2

Preparation Time: 5 minutes

Cooking Time: 5 minutes

Servings: 1-2

INGREDIENTS:

- 2 Oz. Mountain Dew®
- 1 2 Oz. Orange Juice
- 1 Oz. Triple Sec, Cointreau

DIRECTIONS:

1. Add the Cointreau to the juice, and mix well.
2. Add Dew. Have another.

NUTRITION: Calories 15 Protein 21 Fiber 4 Fats 7 Carbohydrates 15

130. Arctic Mouthwash Ice

Preparation Time: 5 minutes

Cooking Time: 5 minutes

Servings: 1-2

INGREDIENTS:

- 5 oz Maui
- 5 oz Mountain Dew

DIRECTIONS:

1. Blend all ingredients in blender until ice is finely crushed, serve immediately.

NUTRITION: Calories 15 Protein 21 Fiber 4 Fats 7 Carbohydrates 15

131. Ass-Smacker

Preparation Time: 5 minutes

Cooking Time: 5 minutes

Servings: 1-2

INGREDIENTS:

- 1 Oz. Key Largo Schnapps
- 4 Oz. Mountain Dew®

DIRECTIONS:

1. Mix and enjoy

NUTRITION: Calories 15 Protein 21 Fiber 4 Fats 7 Carbohydrates 15

132. Captain Dew

Preparation Time: 5 minutes

Cooking Time: 5 minutes

Servings: 1-2

INGREDIENTS:

- 12 Oz. Mountain Dew®
- 4 Oz. Rum, Spiced

DIRECTIONS:

1. Take 16 oz bottle of Mountain Dew® and pour out up to label or if in college drink up to label.
2. Next replenish empty space in bottle about 4oz with captain Morgan.
3. Finally swirl or if chance shake open and drink.

NUTRITION: Calories 15 Protein 21 Fiber 4 Fats 7 Carbohydrates 15

133. Dew Driver

Preparation Time: 5 minutes

Cooking Time: 5 minutes

Servings: 1-2

INGREDIENTS:

- Ice
- 1-part Vodka
- 2 parts Orange Juice
- Mountain Dew to Taste

DIRECTIONS:

1. Add ingredients in any order and enjoy.

NUTRITION: Calories 15 Protein 21 Fiber 4 Fats 7 Carbohydrates 15

134. Ginger Pear Sorbet

Preparation Time: 15 minutes

Cooking Time: 25 minutes

Servings: 1 quart

INGREDIENTS:

- 3 pounds ripe pears
- 1 cup water
- 1 4 teaspoon dried ginger
- 1 tablespoon lemon juice
- ¾ cup sugar

DIRECTIONS:

1. Peel, core, and chop the pears; place with ½ cup of the water and the ginger in a medium-sized covered saucepan. Heat over medium heat, stirring occasionally, for 15–20 minutes, or until very tender.
2. Remove pears from heat and add remaining water, lemon juice, and sugar in a food processor and process until smooth. Refrigerate until thoroughly chilled.
3. Add to ice cream maker and follow manufacturer's instructions for freezing.

NUTRITION: Calories 55 Protein 11 Fiber 4 Fats 37 Carbohydrates 35

135. Lemonade Sorbet

Preparation Time: 15 minutes

Cooking Time: 25 minutes

Servings: 1 Quart

INGREDIENTS:

- 1 cup sugar
- 1 cup water
- 1 cup prepared lemonade
- ¾ cup freshly squeezed lemon juice

DIRECTIONS:

1. Place the sugar and water in a small saucepan, and stir over medium heat until all of the sugar is dissolved. Allow to cool; combine with the lemonade and lemon juice. Cover and refrigerate until cool.
2. Add to ice cream maker and follow manufacturer's instructions for freezing.

NUTRITION: Calories 55 Protein 11 Fiber 4 Fats 37 Carbohydrates 35

136. Lemon Lime Soda Sorbet

Preparation Time: 15 minutes

Cooking Time: 25 minutes

Servings: 1 Quart

INGREDIENTS:

- 1 cup sugar
- 1 (12-ounce) can lemon-lime soda
- 1 cup lemon juice
- 1 cup lime juice

DIRECTIONS:

1. Place the sugar and soda in a small pot, and stir over medium heat until all of the sugar is dissolved. Allow to cool and combine with the lemon and lime juice. Cover and refrigerate until cool.
2. Add to ice cream maker and follow manufacturer's instructions for freezing.

NUTRITION: Calories 55 Protein 11 Fiber 4 Fats 37 Carbohydrates 35

137. Lemon Cream Ice Cream

Preparation Time: 15 minutes

Cooking Time: 25 minutes

Servings: 1 Quart

INGREDIENTS:

- 2 (8-ounce) blocks cream cheese
- 2 cups heavy cream

- ¾ cup sugar
- 1 cup half and half
- 1 tablespoon vanilla extract
- Pinch salt
- Zest and juice from 3 large lemons

DIRECTIONS:
1. Place everything in a blender and blend until smooth.
2. Refrigerate until cold, 4 hours to overnight.
3. Add to ice cream maker and follow manufacturer's instructions for freezing.

NUTRITION: Calories 55 Protein 11 Fiber 4 Fats 37 Carbohydrates 35

138. Mascarpone Ice Cream

Preparation Time: 15 minutes

Cooking Time: 25 minutes

Servings: 1 Quart

INGREDIENTS:

- 1 cup whole milk
- 1½ cups heavy cream
- 4 large egg yolks
- ¾ cup sugar
- Pinch salt
- 1 tablespoon limoncello
- 1 tablespoon candied lemon peel, minced (see Candied Citrus Peels, Chapter 17)
- 8 ounces mascarpone, softened

DIRECTIONS:

1. In a medium saucepan, bring milk and cream to a boil and set aside.

2. In a medium bowl, whisk together egg yolks, sugar, and salt until thick and lighter in color.

3. Slowly stream hot milk mixture into egg mixture until fully incorporated. Add egg mixture to saucepan and cook over medium heat until thick, being careful not to boil. Strain into a clean bowl; add limoncello, and refrigerate 4 hours to overnight.

4. Stir in mascarpone. Add to ice cream maker and follow manufacturer's instructions for freezing. Fold in minced candied lemon peel before placing in the freezer.

NUTRITION: Calories 55 Protein 11 Fiber 4 Fats 37 Carbohydrates 35

139. Red Velvet Cake Ice Cream

Preparation Time: 15 minutes

Cooking Time: 25 minutes

Servings: 1 Quart

INGREDIENTS:

- 1 cup heavy cream
- 1 cup half and half
- 1 vanilla bean, split, seeded, and pod saved for another use
- 6 ounces white chocolate
- ¾ cup sugar
- Pinch salt
- 4 egg yolks
- 12 ounces cream cheese, softened and cubed
- 1 tablespoon lemon juice
- ½ cup red velvet cake, cubed into ½ cubes and frozen solid

DIRECTIONS:

1. Bring cream, half and half, and vanilla seeds to a boil. Place white chocolate in a large bowl. Pour cream mixture over white chocolate. Allow to sit for 2 minutes, then stir until smooth.

2. Whisk sugar, salt, and egg yolks until thick and lighter in color.

3. Slowly stream hot cream mixture into egg mixture until fully incorporated. Add egg mixture to pan and cook over medium heat until thick, being careful not to boil. Strain into a clean bowl; stir in cream cheese until completely incorporated and smooth. Stir in lemon juice and refrigerate 4 hours to overnight.

4. Add to ice cream maker and follow manufacturer's instructions for freezing. Fold in frozen cake cubes before placing in the freezer.

NUTRITION: Calories 55 Protein 11 Fiber 4 Fats 37 Carbohydrates 35

140. Raspberry Dark Chocolate Swirl Ice Cream

Preparation Time: 15 minutes

Cooking Time: 25 minutes

Servings: 1 Quart

INGREDIENTS:

- 1 cup half and half
- 1 cup sugar
- Pinch salt
- 4 large egg yolks
- ½ cup heavy cream
- 1¾ cups raspberry purée, seeds strained out
- 2 teaspoons vanilla extract
- Generous squeeze fresh lemon juice
- 1½ cups Dark Chocolate Fudge Sauce

DIRECTIONS:

1. In a small saucepan, combine the half and half, sugar, and salt. Stir over medium heat. Once simmering, remove from heat and set aside.
2. In a separate bowl, whisk egg yolks. If needed, reheat milk mixture until hot, and temper the yolks by adding half of the mixture into the eggs, whisking constantly. Add egg mixture to the saucepan, and heat until thickened.
3. Pour heavy cream into a large mixing bowl over an ice bath. Strain custard into the cream, stirring until cooled. Add raspberry purée, vanilla extract, and lemon juice. Stir, and place in refrigerator until thoroughly chilled, about 5 hours or overnight.
4. Once chilled, add to ice cream maker and follow manufacturer's instructions for freezing. Just before storing in the freezer, quickly and loosely swirl in the Dark Chocolate Fudge Sauce.

NUTRITION: Calories 55 Protein 11 Fiber 4 Fats 37 Carbohydrates 35

141. Banana Frozen Yogurt

Preparation Time: 15 minutes

Cooking Time: 25 minutes

Servings: 1 Quart

INGREDIENTS:

- 3 large ripe bananas, smashed
- 3 cups plain whole-milk yogurt
- 1 4 cup light corn syrup
- 2 teaspoons vanilla extract
- 2 teaspoons lemon juice

DIRECTIONS:

1. Place all ingredients in a blender or food processor, and blend until smooth.
2. Add to ice cream maker and follow manufacturer's instructions for freezing.

NUTRITION: Calories 55 Protein 11 Fiber 4 Fats 37 Carbohydrates 35

142. Zesty Lemon Frozen Yogurt

Preparation Time: 15 minutes

Cooking Time: 25 minutes

Servings: 1 Quart

INGREDIENTS:

- 2 cups Greek yogurt
- 2 cups plain whole-milk yogurt
- ¾ cup sugar
- ½ cup light corn syrup
- 1 4 cup fresh lemon juice
- 2 tablespoons lemon zest

DIRECTIONS:
1. Place all ingredients in a blender or food processor, and blend until smooth.
2. Add to ice cream maker and follow manufacturer's instructions for freezing.

NUTRITION: Calories 55 Protein 11 Fiber 4 Fats 37 Carbohydrates 35

143. Blueberry Frozen Yogurt

Preparation Time: 15 minutes

Cooking Time: 25 minutes

Servings: 1 Quart

INGREDIENTS:

- 4 cups blueberries
- Juice and zest of ½ lemon
- ¾ cup sugar
- 1 cup Greek yogurt
- 1 teaspoon vanilla extract

DIRECTIONS:
1. In a small bowl, combine the blueberries, lemon juice and zest, and sugar. Stir and allow to macerate at room temperature for 1–2 hours.
2. After blueberries are ready, place all ingredients in a blender or food processor, and blend until smooth.
3. Add to ice cream maker and follow manufacturer's instructions for freezing.

NUTRITION: Calories 55 Protein 11 Fiber 4 Fats 37 Carbohydrates 35

144. Strawberry Frozen Yogurt

Preparation Time: 15 minutes

Cooking Time: 25 minutes

Servings: 1 Quart

INGREDIENTS:

- 4 cups strawberries
- Juice and zest of ½ lemon
- 1 cup sugar
- 1 cup Greek yogurt
- 1 teaspoon vanilla extract

DIRECTIONS:

1. In a small bowl, combine the strawberries, lemon juice and zest, and sugar. Stir and allow to macerate at room temperature for 1–2 hours.
2. After strawberries are ready, place all ingredients in a blender or food processor, and blend until smooth.
3. Add to ice cream maker and follow manufacturer's instructions for freezing.

NUTRITION: Calories 55 Protein 11 Fiber 4 Fats 37 Carbohydrates 35

145. Limoncello Gelato (Gelato Di Limoncello)

Preparation Time: 15 minutes

Cooking Time: 25 minutes

Servings: 1 Quart

INGREDIENTS:

- 3 cups whole milk
- 1 cup sugar
- Pinch salt
- Zest of 2 lemons, finely chopped
- 5 large egg yolks
- 2 third cup heavy cream
- 1 4 cup limoncello
- Fresh-squeezed juice of ½ lemon

DIRECTIONS:

1. In a small saucepan, combine the milk, sugar, salt, and lemon zest. Stir over medium heat. Once simmering, remove from heat, cover, and allow too steep for 1 hour.
2. Reheat milk mixture over medium-low heat.
3. In a separate bowl, whisk egg yolks. Once milk mixture is hot, temper the yolks by adding half of the mixture into the eggs, whisking constantly. Return mixture to saucepan, and heat until thickened. Pour ½ cup of heavy cream into a large mixing bowl over an ice bath. Strain custard into the cream.

4. Stir together limoncello, lemon juice, and remaining cream. Stir into gelato mixture. Refrigerate 8 hours to overnight.
5. Add to ice cream maker and follow manufacturer's instructions for freezing. Stop the churning as soon as the gelato is just frozen.

NUTRITION: Calories 55 Protein 11 Fiber 4 Fats 37 Carbohydrates 35

146. Fresh Fig Gelato (Gelato Di Fiche)

Preparation Time: 15 minutes

Cooking Time: 25 minutes

Servings: 1 Quart

INGREDIENTS:

- 1-pound fresh figs, peeled
- Juice and zest of ½ lemon
- 1 4 cup honey

DIRECTIONS:

1. In small bowl, combine the peeled figs, lemon juice, and honey. Stir and allow to macerate at room temperature for 1–2 hours.
2. After figs are ready, place all ingredients in a blender or food processor, and blend until smooth.
3. Add to ice cream maker and follow manufacturer's instructions for freezing. Stop the churning as soon as the gelato is just frozen.

NUTRITION: Calories 55 Protein 11 Fiber 4 Fats 37 Carbohydrates 35

147. Black Cherry Ice Cream

Preparation Time: 15 minutes

Cooking Time: 25 minutes

Servings: 1 Quart

INGREDIENTS:

- 1-pound black cherries, pitted and chopped
- 2 teaspoons lemon juice
- 1¾ cups whole milk
- 2 cups heavy cream
- 4 large egg yolks
- 1 cup sugar
- 2 teaspoons vanilla extract
- 2 drops almond extract

DIRECTIONS:

1. Toss the chopped cherries with lemon juice and set aside.
2. In a medium to large saucepan, combine the milk and cream, and stir over medium heat.

3. In a separate bowl, whisk egg yolks with the sugar until thick and foamy. Once milk mixture is hot, temper the yolks by adding half of the mixture into the eggs, whisking constantly. Return mixture to saucepan, and heat until thickened.
4. Add three-quarters of the reserved cherries to the saucepan, cook for 10 minutes, and then remove from heat. Allow to cool for 15 minutes, then add vanilla and almond extracts.
5. Place mixture into a blender. Purée until smooth. Place in refrigerator until thoroughly chilled, about 5 hours or overnight.
6. Once chilled, add to ice cream maker and follow manufacturer's instructions for freezing. Near the end of the freezing cycle, add remaining cherries and allow to mix.

NUTRITION: Calories 55 Protein 11 Fiber 4 Fats 37 Carbohydrates 35

148. Lemon Ice Cream

Preparation Time: 15 minutes

Cooking Time: 25 minutes

Servings: 1 Quart

INGREDIENTS:

- Zest of 4 lemons
- ¾ cup sugar
- ¾ cup milk
- 21 4 cups heavy cream
- Pinch salt
- 4 large egg yolks
- ½ teaspoon lemon extract

DIRECTIONS:

1. Combine the lemon zest and sugar with your fingers until aromatic and well combined. In a small saucepan, combine the lemon sugar mixture, milk, 2 third cup of the cream, and salt. Stir over medium heat. Once simmering, remove from heat, cover, and allow to step for 1 hour.
2. After 1 hour, reheat milk mixture over medium-low heat.
3. In a separate bowl, whisk egg yolks. Once milk mixture is hot, temper the yolks by adding half of the mixture into the eggs, whisking constantly. Return mixture to saucepan, and heat until thickened.
4. Pour rest of the heavy cream and lemon extract into a large mixing bowl over an ice bath. Strain lemon custard into the cream, discarding the zest, and stir until cooled. Place in refrigerator until thoroughly chilled, about 5 hours or overnight.
5. Once chilled, add to ice cream maker and follow manufacturer's instructions for freezing.

NUTRITION: Calories 55 Protein 11 Fiber 4 Fats 37 Carbohydrates 35

149. Italian Espresso Ice Cream

Preparation Time: 15 minutes

Cooking Time: 25 minutes

Servings: 1 Quart

INGREDIENTS:

- 1 ½ cups of whole milk
- 1 1 4 cups of granulated sugar
- 3 cups of heavy cream
- 1 cup of freshly brewed dark Italian espresso, fully cooled

DIRECTION:

1. Make sure your freezer is set at or below 0 degrees Fahrenheit (-18 degrees Celsius). Place the ice cream bowl attachment in the freezer for at least 15 hours.
2. Check that the ice cream bowl is completely frozen by giving it a shake before use. If you hear no movement, the bowl's cooling liquid is properly frozen.
3. Using your stand mixer and a mixing bowl, combine the milk and sugar, at a low speed until the sugar is fully dissolved in the milk.
4. Stir in the brewed and cooled espresso and the heavy cream. Stir thoroughly until all ingredients are evenly blended. Refrigerate for 1-2 hours.
5. Take the ice cream freezer bowl out of the freezer and set it on the middle of your stand mixer's base.
6. Slide the assembly drive onto the bottom of the mixer head. Fit the dasher into the bowl and connect to the assembly drive.
7. When your stand mixer is prepared, switch it into "Level 1" or "Stir" mode. The dasher will begin to turn in the bowl. Pour the refrigerated mixture immediately from the mixing bowl into the freezer bowl.
8. After approximately 25-30 minutes, the mixture will have frozen to a thick, creamy soft-serve consistency. Serve directly from the ice cream freezer bowl into serving bowls or cones, and enjoy!
9. For a more hard-frozen consistency, transfer the mixture from the freezer bowl into an air-tight container and keep in the freezer for at least 2 more hours.

NUTRITION: Calories 55 Protein 11 Fiber 4 Fats 37 Carbohydrates 35

150. Sangria Slushies

Preparation Time: 15 minutes

Cooking Time: 25 minutes

Servings: 1 Quart

Ingredients:

- 2 cups of red table wine
- 1 cup of brandy
- ½ cup of triple sec
- 1 ½ cups of lemon juice (bottled or freshly squeezed, unsweetened)
- 1 ½ cups of orange juice (bottled or freshly squeezed, unsweetened)

- 1 cup of white sugar
- ½ cup of concentrated lemonade
- ½ cup of orange slices, cut into bite-sized chunks
- ½ cup of lemon slices, cut into bite-sized chunks
- ½ cup of lime slices, cut into bite-sized chunks

DIRECTION:

1. Make sure your freezer is set at or below 0 degrees Fahrenheit (-18 degrees Celsius). Place the ice cream bowl attachment in the freezer for at least 15 hours.
2. Check that the ice cream bowl is completely frozen by giving it a shake before use. If you hear no movement, the bowl's cooling liquid is properly frozen.
3. Using your stand mixer and a mixing bowl, combine the lemon juice, concentrated lemonade, orange juice, and sugar. Stir thoroughly, until the sugar is fully dissolved and all ingredients are completely blended.
4. Add the triple sec, brandy, and red wine. Again, stir thoroughly until all ingredients are thoroughly blended.
5. Take the ice cream freezer bowl out of the freezer and set it on the middle of your stand mixer's base.
6. Slide the assembly drive onto the bottom of the mixer head. Fit the dasher into the bowl and connect to the assembly drive.
7. When your stand mixer is prepared, switch it into "Level 1" or "Stir" mode. The dasher will begin to turn in the bowl. Pour the refrigerated mixture immediately from the mixing bowl into the freezer bowl.
8. After approximately 25-30 minutes (in the last five minutes of freezing), add the chunks of orange, lemon and lime into the freezer bowl to let mix completely. allow to freeze another 5 minutes.
9. After approximately 30 minutes (total), the sangria will have frozen to a thick, slushy consistency, with the fruit blended and lightly frozen perfectly throughout. Transfer from the freezer bowl into glasses or a pitcher, and enjoy!

NUTRITION: Calories 55 Protein 11 Fiber 4 Fats 37 Carbohydrates 35

151. Lemon Custard Sorbet

Preparation Time: 15 minutes

Cooking Time: 25 minutes

Servings: 1 Quart

INGREDIENTS:

- 1 whole vanilla bean
- 2 cups of filtered water
- 2 cups of granulated sugar
- 2 1 4 cups of freshly squeezed lemon juice
- 1 ½ tablespoons of finely diced zest of lemon
- 1 4 cup of fat free powdered milk
- 1 cup of heavy cream
- 1 ½ teaspoon of pure vanilla extract

DIRECTION:

1. Make sure your freezer is set at or below 0 degrees Fahrenheit (-18 degrees Celsius). Place the ice cream bowl attachment in the freezer for at least 15 hours.
2. Check that the ice cream bowl is completely frozen by giving it a shake before use. If you hear no movement, the bowl's cooling liquid is properly frozen.
3. In a large saucepan, mix the sugar and water and bring to a low boil over medium to high heat.
4. Using a sharp knife, split the vanilla bean down the middle length wise, then use the blunt end of the knife to scrape out the seeds of the bean.
5. Stir the seeds and the bean pod into the heating sugar and water. Lower the heat and continue to simmer on low heat, without stirring, until the sugar has fully dissolved, about 3-5 minutes.
6. Extract the vanilla bean pod and discard it.
7. Remove the mixture from heat and allow to cool completely. This simple syrup can be pre-made and refrigerated ahead of time when making the sorbet. Refrigerate until ready to move onto next steps.
8. Add the lemon juice, vanilla extract, powdered milk, cream, and lemon zest to the cooled simple syrup, and stir to combine fully. Refrigerate for 1-2 hours.
9. Take the ice cream freezer bowl out of the freezer and set it on the middle of your stand mixer's base.
10. Slide the assembly drive onto the bottom of the mixer head. Fit the dasher into the bowl and connect to the assembly drive.
11. When your stand mixer is prepared, switch it into "Level 1" or "Stir" mode. The dasher will begin to turn in the bowl. Pour the refrigerated sorbet mixture immediately from the mixing bowl into the freezer bowl.
12. After approximately 30 minutes, the mixture will have frozen to a thick, soft icy consistency. Serve directly from the ice cream freezer bowl, and enjoy!
13. For a more hard-frozen consistency, transfer the sorbet mixture from the freezer bowl into an air-tight container and keep in the freezer for at least 2 more hours.

NUTRITION: Calories 55 Protein 11 Fiber 4 Fats 37 Carbohydrates 35

152. Plum Sorbet

Preparation Time: 15 minutes

Cooking Time: 25 minutes

Servings: 1 Quart

INGREDIENTS:

- 3 pounds of fresh ripe plums, peeled and sliced into cubes with the pits discarded
- 1 cup of filtered water
- 1 cup of white sugar
- 1 tablespoon of corn syrup

DIRECTION:

1. Make sure your freezer is set at or below 0 degrees Fahrenheit (-18 degrees Celsius). Place the ice cream bowl attachment in the freezer for at least 15 hours.
2. Check that the ice cream bowl is completely frozen by giving it a shake before use. If you hear no movement, the bowl's cooling liquid is properly frozen.

3. In a large saucepan, mix the sugar and water and bring to a low boil over medium to high heat.

4. Lower the heat and continue to simmer the sugar and water, on low heat, without stirring, until the sugar has fully dissolved, about 3-5 minutes.

5. Remove from heat, transfer to a mixing bowl, and allow to cool completely. This simple syrup can be pre-made and refrigerated ahead of time when making sorbet. Refrigerate until ready to move onto next steps.

6. Place the plums into a food processor or blender, and blend until completely smooth and fully pureed.

7. Pour the processed puree through a fine mesh sieve and discard the pulp.

8. Using your stand mixer and a mixing bowl, combine the smoothly processed plum puree with the corn syrup and cooled simple syrup. Stir until all ingredients are evenly combined.

9. Cover and refrigerate for at least 2 hours.

10. Take the ice cream freezer bowl out of the freezer and set it on the middle of your stand mixer's base.

11. Slide the assembly drive onto the bottom of the mixer head. Fit the dasher into the bowl and connect to the assembly drive.

12. When your stand mixer is prepared, switch it into "Level 1" or "Stir" mode. The dasher will begin to turn in the bowl. Pour the refrigerated sorbet mixture immediately from the mixing bowl into the freezer bowl.

13. After approximately 25-30 minutes, the mixture will have frozen to a thick, slushy consistency. Serve directly from the ice cream freezer bowl, and enjoy!

14. For a more hard-frozen consistency, transfer the sorbet mixture from the freezer bowl into an air-tight container and keep in the freezer for at least 2 more hours.

NUTRITION: Calories 55 Protein 11 Fiber 4 Fats 37 Carbohydrates 35

153. Mascarpone Sorbet

Preparation Time: 15 minutes

Cooking Time: 25 minutes

Servings: 1 Quart

INGREDIENTS:

- 2 pounds of whipped mascarpone cheese (sometimes sold as "Italian cream cheese")
- 1 ½ cups of filtered water
- 1 ½ cups of extra-fine white confectioners' white sugar
- ¾ cup of lemon juice (fresh squeezed or bottled, as long as it's unsweetened)

DIRECTION:

1. Make sure your freezer is set at or below 0 degrees Fahrenheit (-18 degrees Celsius). Place the ice cream bowl attachment in the freezer for at least 15 hours.

2. Check that the ice cream bowl is completely frozen by giving it a shake before use. If you hear no movement, the bowl's cooling liquid is properly frozen.

3. In a large saucepan, mix the sugar and water and bring to a low boil over medium to high heat.

4. Lower the heat and continue to simmer the sugar and water, on low heat, without stirring, until the sugar has fully dissolved, about 3-5 minutes.

5. Remove from heat, transfer to a mixing bowl, and allow to cool completely. This simple syrup can be pre-made and refrigerated ahead of time when making sorbet. Refrigerate until ready to move onto next steps.

6. Using your stand mixer and a mixing bowl, whip the mascarpone cheese together with the lemon juice, until fully combined and fluffy.

7. Combine the whipped mascarpone and lemon juice with the cooled simple syrup. Stir until all ingredients are evenly combined.

8. Cover and refrigerate for at least 2 hours.

9. Take the ice cream freezer bowl out of the freezer and set it on the middle of your stand mixer's base.

10. Slide the assembly drive onto the bottom of the mixer head. Fit the dasher into the bowl and connect to the assembly drive.

11. When your stand mixer is prepared, switch it into "Level 1" or "Stir" mode. The dasher will begin to turn in the bowl. Pour the refrigerated sorbet mixture immediately from the mixing bowl into the freezer bowl.

12. After approximately 25-30 minutes, the mixture will have frozen to a thick, dense, creamy consistency. Serve directly from the ice cream freezer bowl, and enjoy!

13. For a more hard-frozen consistency, transfer the sorbet mixture from the freezer bowl into an air-tight container and keep in the freezer for at least 2 more hours.

NUTRITION: Calories 45 Protein 13 Fiber 2 Fats 17 Carbohydrates 45

154. Sweet Cherry Sorbet

Preparation Time: 15 minutes

Cooking Time: 25 minutes

Servings: 1 Quart

INGREDIENTS:

- 3 pounds of fresh ripe cherries, with the pits and stems discarded
- 1 cup of filtered water
- 1 cup of white sugar
- ½ cup of lemon juice (fresh squeezed or bottled, as long as it's unsweetened)

DIRECTION:

1. Make sure your freezer is set at or below 0 degrees Fahrenheit (-18 degrees Celsius). Place the ice cream bowl attachment in the freezer for at least 15 hours.

2. Check that the ice cream bowl is completely frozen by giving it a shake before use. If you hear no movement, the bowl's cooling liquid is properly frozen.

3. In a large saucepan, mix the sugar and water and bring to a low boil over medium to high heat.

4. Lower the heat and continue to simmer the sugar and water, on low heat, without stirring, until the sugar has fully dissolved, about 3-5 minutes.

5. Remove from heat, transfer to a mixing bowl, and allow to cool completely. This simple syrup can be pre-made and refrigerated ahead of time when making sorbet. Refrigerate until ready to move onto next steps.

6. Place the cherries into a food processor or blender, and blend until completely smooth and fully pureed.

7. Pour the processed puree through a fine mesh sieve and discard the skins and any pulp.

8. Using your stand mixer and a mixing bowl, combine the smoothly processed cherry puree with the lemon juice and cooled simple syrup. Stir until all ingredients are evenly combined.

9. Cover and refrigerate for at least 2 hours.

10. Take the ice cream freezer bowl out of the freezer and set it on the middle of your stand mixer's base.

11. Slide the assembly drive onto the bottom of the mixer head. Fit the dasher into the bowl and connect to the assembly drive.

12. When your stand mixer is prepared, switch it into "Level 1" or "Stir" mode. The dasher will begin to turn in the bowl. Pour the refrigerated sorbet mixture immediately from the mixing bowl into the freezer bowl.

13. After approximately 25-30 minutes, the mixture will have frozen to a thick, slushy consistency. Serve directly from the ice cream freezer bowl, and enjoy!

14. For a more hard-frozen consistency, transfer the sorbet mixture from the freezer bowl into an air-tight container and keep in the freezer for at least 2 more hours.

NUTRITION: Calories 45 Protein 13 Fiber 2 Fats 17 Carbohydrates 45

155. All-Natural Pink Lemonade Sorbet

Preparation Time: 25 minutes

Cooking Time: 35 minutes

Servings: 1 Quart

INGREDIENTS:

- 3 cups of filtered water
- 3 cups of granulated sugar
- 2 ½ cups of fresh strawberries, rinsed and patted dry
- 2 1 4 cups of freshly squeezed lemon juice
- 1 ½ tablespoons of finely diced zest of lemon

DIRECTION:

1. Make sure your freezer is set at or below 0 degrees Fahrenheit (-18 degrees Celsius). Place the ice cream bowl attachment in the freezer for at least 15 hours.

2. Check that the ice cream bowl is completely frozen by giving it a shake before use. If you hear no movement, the bowl's cooling liquid is properly frozen.

3. In a food processor or blender, puree the strawberries until quite smooth, then strain the strawberry juice through a fine mesh sieve and discard the seeds and husks. Set aside the approximately 1 ½ cups of strawberry juice that will have strained through.

4. In a large saucepan, mix the sugar and water and bring to a low boil over medium to high heat.

5. Lower the heat and continue to simmer the sugar and water, on low heat, without stirring, until the sugar has fully dissolved, about 3-5 minutes.

6. Remove from heat and allow to cool completely. This simple syrup can be pre-made and refrigerated ahead of time when making sorbet. Refrigerate about 2 hours or until ready to move onto next steps.

7. Add the reserved strawberry juice, and the lemon juice and zest, to the cooled simple syrup, and stir to combine fully. Chill in the refrigerator for 1-2 hours.

8. Take the ice cream freezer bowl out of the freezer and set it on the middle of your stand mixer's base.

9. Slide the assembly drive onto the bottom of the mixer head. Fit the dasher into the bowl and connect to the assembly drive.

10. When your stand mixer is prepared, switch it into "Level 1" or "Stir" mode. The dasher will begin to turn in the bowl. Pour the refrigerated sorbet mixture immediately from the mixing bowl into the freezer bowl.

11. After approximately 30 minutes, the mixture will have frozen to a thick, soft icy consistency. Serve directly from the ice cream freezer bowl, and enjoy!

12. For a more hard-frozen consistency, transfer the sorbet mixture from the freezer bowl into an air-tight container and keep in the freezer for at least 2 more hours.

NUTRITION: Calories 45Protein 13 Fiber 2 Fats 17 Carbohydrates 45

156. Fresh Strawberry Ice Cream

Preparation Time: 25 minutes

Cooking Time: 35 minutes

Servings: 1 Quart

INGREDIENTS:

- 3 cups of fresh ripe strawberries, rinsed and patted dry, sliced with the stems removed
- 4 tablespoons of freshly squeezed lemon juice
- 1 ½ cups of white sugar
- 1 ½ cups of whole milk
- 2 ¾ cups of heavy cream
- 1 ½ teaspoons of pure vanilla extract

DIRECTION:

1. Make sure your freezer is set at or below 0 degrees Fahrenheit (-18 degrees Celsius). Place the ice cream bowl attachment in the freezer for at least 15 hours.

2. Check that the ice cream bowl is completely frozen by giving it a shake before use. If you hear no movement, the bowl's cooling liquid is properly frozen.

3. Using your stand mixer and a mixing bowl, stir the sliced strawberries, the lemon juice, and ½ cup of the sugar.

4. Stir until strawberries are fully coated and the lemon juice and sugar are evenly blended, then leave to sit so that the strawberries can soak up the lemon and sugar for approximately two hours.

5. Strain the berries in a fine mesh sieve and conserve the juice.

6. Using a hand-masher, food processor or blender, mash or puree half of the berries until quite smooth.

7. Using your stand mixer and a mixing bowl, stir the milk with the remaining sugar until the sugar is fully dissolved.

8. Stir in the vanilla extract, the heavy cream, the reserved berry juice and the mashed berries, stirring thoroughly until all ingredients are evenly combined. Place the mixture in the refrigerator for 2 hours.

9. Take the ice cream freezer bowl out of the freezer and set it on the middle of your stand mixer's base.

10. Slide the assembly drive onto the bottom of the mixer head. Fit the dasher into the bowl and connect to the assembly drive.

11. When your stand mixer is prepared, switch it into "Level 1" or "Stir" mode. The dasher will begin to turn in the bowl. Pour the refrigerated mixture immediately from the mixing bowl into the freezer bowl.

12. After approximately 20 minutes (in the last five minutes of freezing), add the reserved sliced and strained strawberries into the ice cream bowl to let mix completely.

13. After approximately 25-30 minutes (total), the mixture will have frozen to a thick, creamy soft-serve consistency, with the frozen berry slices packed with juicy goodness. Serve directly from the ice cream freezer bowl into serving bowls or cones, and enjoy!

14. For a more hard-frozen consistency, transfer the mixture from the freezer bowl into an air-tight container and keep in the freezer for at least 2 more hours.

NUTRITION: Calories 45 Protein 13 Fiber 2 Fats 17 Carbohydrates 45

157. Tarragon Sorbet

Preparation Time: 25 minutes

Cooking Time: 35 minutes

Servings: 1 Quart

INGREDIENTS:

- 1 tablespoon of dried ground tarragon
- 1 4 cup of unsweetened lemon juice (either fresh or bottled is fine)
- 1 ½ cups of filtered water
- 1 ½ cups of white sugar
- 1 tablespoon of corn syrup

DIRECTION:

1. Make sure your freezer is set at or below 0 degrees Fahrenheit (-18 degrees Celsius). Place the ice cream bowl attachment in the freezer for at least 15 hours.

2. Check that the ice cream bowl is completely frozen by giving it a shake before use. If you hear no movement, the bowl's cooling liquid is properly frozen.

3. In a large saucepan, mix the sugar and water and bring to a boil over medium to high heat.

4. Lower the heat and continue to simmer the sugar and water, on low heat, without stirring, until the sugar has fully dissolved, about 3-5 minutes.

5. Remove from heat, transfer to a mixing bowl, and allow to cool completely. This simple syrup can be pre-made and refrigerated ahead of time when making sorbet. Refrigerate until ready to move onto next steps.

6. Using your stand mixer and a mixing bowl, combine the tarragon, lemon juice, corn syrup, and cooled simple syrup. Mix until all ingredients are evenly combined.

7. Cover and refrigerate for at least 2 hours.

8. Take the ice cream freezer bowl out of the freezer and set it on the middle of your stand mixer's base.

9. Slide the assembly drive onto the bottom of the mixer head. Fit the dasher into the bowl and connect to the assembly drive.

10. When your stand mixer is prepared, switch it into "Level 1" or "Stir" mode. The dasher will begin to turn in the bowl. Pour the refrigerated mixture immediately from the mixing bowl into the freezer bowl.

11. After approximately 25-30 minutes, the mixture will have frozen to a thick, slushy consistency. Serve directly from the ice cream freezer bowl, and enjoy!

12. For a more hard-frozen consistency, transfer the sorbet mixture from the freezer bowl into an air-tight container and keep in the freezer for at least 2 more hours.

NUTRITION: Calories 45 Protein 13 Fiber 2 Fats 17 Carbohydrates 45

158. Cool And Classic Lemon Sorbet

Preparation Time: 25 minutes

Cooking Time: 35 minutes

Servings: 1 Quart

INGREDIENTS:

- 3 cups of filtered water
- 3 cups of granulated sugar
- 2 1 4 cups of freshly squeezed lemon juice
- 1 ½ tablespoons of finely diced zest of lemon

DIRECTION:

1. Make sure your freezer is set at or below 0 degrees Fahrenheit (-18 degrees Celsius). Place the ice cream bowl attachment in the freezer for at least 15 hours.

2. Check that the ice cream bowl is completely frozen by giving it a shake before use. If you hear no movement, the bowl's cooling liquid is properly frozen.

3. In a large saucepan, mix the sugar and water and bring to a low boil over medium to high heat.

4. Lower the heat and continue to simmer the sugar and water, on low heat, without stirring, until the sugar has fully dissolved, about 3-5 minutes.

5. Remove from heat and allow to cool completely. This simple syrup can be pre-made and refrigerated ahead of time when making sorbet. Refrigerate until ready to move onto next steps.

6. Add the lemon juice and zest to the cooled simple syrup, and stir to combine fully.

7. Take the ice cream freezer bowl out of the freezer and set it on the middle of your stand mixer's base.

8. Slide the assembly drive onto the bottom of the mixer head. Fit the dasher into the bowl and connect to the assembly drive.

9. When your stand mixer is prepared, switch it into "Level 1" or "Stir" mode. The dasher will begin to turn in the bowl. Pour the sorbet mixture immediately from the mixing bowl into the freezer bowl.

10. After approximately 25-30 minutes, the mixture will have frozen to a thick, soft icy consistency. Serve directly from the ice cream freezer bowl, and enjoy!

NUTRITION: Calories 45 Protein 13 Fiber 2 Fats 17 Carbohydrates 45

CONCLUSION

Congratulations! You have reached the end of this cookbook and deserve a big round of applause. Hopefully, you walked away, learning something new about working with the new cooking tools. I hope this book was able to help you create flavorful southern dishes in the kitchen that embodies the essence of American comfort food. The next step is to mix and match lunch and dinner recipes to come up with a new menu for you and your family to enjoy.

I know that you and the people who share your life with enjoy these recipes for years to come, and it has been a pleasure for me to make these recipes available in this collection. If you need to cook a great dish, keep this book handy, and you'll never run out of delicious recipes. I hope you enjoyed the book and all the delicious recipes it has offered you.

You can use the summer months to enjoy crab dishes and grilled fish. Spring and summer offer a bounty of local seafood and fresh produce.

You can use the cooler months to make gumbo, jambalaya, and other soups whose recipes are native to the area. They will warm your family up and have them asking for more. You can use the basics in this book to help you tackle all kinds of recipes from Louisiana, and the experience will give you more confidence in cooking the many intricate dishes of the area. It is time to celebrate the wonderful cuisine of this area.

Step away from your favorite takeout. Spend a day in the kitchen, and make these enticing recipes yourself.

The time and effort you put in will pay off, and you'll have a fun time too!

You can consult several cookbooks and online resources to learn more about Louisiana's rich culinary traditions. Louisiana Cookin', The Root Cellar Cookbook, and Big Easy Cookbook are wonderful resources that can help you dive into the true core of Louisiana's cuisine.

This diet involves healthy grains, vegetables, fruits, olive oil, beans, and proteins like seafood and fish. Red meat is unusually absorbed and reasonably only once a week or even a fortnight.

This diet concentrates on foods and natural recipes of the Mediterranean method of cooking. While the Mediterranean food is not your standard, common diet, it is absolutely a lifestyle. You can think of it as a different way of eating and living. Following this lifestyle, you are able to make well-balanced meals decisions that promote your health and taste exceptional while advancing weight loss and the development of lean muscle.

Once again, thank you for ready my story. I am glad u stayed till the end. And I'm glad to hear you liked it. It took me a while to write that one. I hope you will enjoy it. Thank you for the great comment. I don't show my writing in public, and hence the full story is below. More stories to come; until then, enjoy and have a great day.

CPSIA information can be obtained
at www.ICGtesting.com
Printed in the USA
LVHW061002220321
681561LV00068B/320